FRIENDS AND RELATIONS was performed for the first time at The Abbey Theatre, Dublin, on Monday, the 30th of June, 1941. It was produced by Frank Dermody with the following cast:

KATE, May Craig.

FANNY CAIRNS, Ria Mooney

DOREEN CAIRNS, Brid Ni Loingsigh.

ARTHUR CAIRNS, Gerard Healy.

ADAM BOTHWELL, Denis O'Dea.

JENNY CONN, Eithne Dunn.

EDWARD SCANTLEBURY, F. J. McCormick.

MRS. CORKEN, Eileen Crowe.

GOURLAY, Fred Johnson.

CHARACTERS

KATE, Sir Samuel's Lepper's servant.

FANNY CAIRNS, his niece.

ARTHUR, her son.

EDWARD SCANTLEBURY, her brother, Sir Samuel's nephew.

DOREEN, her daughter.

ADAM BOTHWELL, Sir Samuel's second cousin.

MRS. CORKEN, Sir Samuel's sister.

JAMES FINLAY, Sir Samuel's solicitor.

JENNY CONN.

JOHN JAMES GOURLAY, Sir Samuel's gardener.

The scene is laid in the morning-room of Sir Samuel Lepper's mansion, Slieve Bearnagh House, at Stormont, outside Belfast.

The time is the present.

FRIENDS AND RELATIONS

ACT I

The blinds are drawn in the morning-room of Sir Samuel Lepper's mansion, Slieve Bearnagh House, at Stormont, outside Belfast; for Sir Samuel was buried early this afternoon. If it were not for the drawn blinds, brilliant sunshine would be streaming through the windows, but even, drawn as they are, the sun dispels some of the darkness and lightens the look of the heavy, dull and very ugly furniture. There is scarcely a piece in the room which was not purchased by Sir Samuel's parents when they were engaged to be married, and he liked it as much as they did. It gave him a sense of solidity, and all the Leppers liked solidity. When Sir Samuel surveyed this room, or, indeed, any room in Slieve Bearnagh House, he saw signs of permanence, of abiding things, of inherited and heritable property. "There's none of your flimsy-flamsy stuff in this house," he frequently remarked with pride; and, indeed, he was right: there wasn't. The furniture, which is over eighty years old, is as substantial now as it was on the day it was bought, and it will still be substantial eighty years hence.

What will happen to it, if it is ever removed from Slieve Bearnagh House, is impossible to foretell. Houses large enough to accommodate vast sideboards and enormous tables are no longer built. It is doomed, no doubt, to fill the wide empty spaces in hotels and old-fashioned boarding-houses. Those great chairs, almost large enough to be beds, which filled Miss Letitia Crombie, commonly called "Teeshie," with elation when she and young Lawrence Lepper were spending their afternoons in the shop at Castle Junction where they bought their household goods, will shed their romantic associations and become practical

9

furnishings in a home from home at Ballycastle or Warrenpoint. Well, that's all over! Mr. and Mrs. Lawrence Lepper were buried long ago in the family vault at Dundonald, and there, this afternoon, their son, Sir Samuel Lepper, " in the presence of a large and representative concourse of friends and relations," was reverently laid beside them. His wife, Cassie, had been laid there fifteen years earlier. Long before that, their only child, a boy of ten, was laid in it, too. There is a lot of Lepper earth in Dundonald.

Slieve Bearnagh House is beginning to look as if it were on its last legs. The city, which was remote when it was built, has crept all round it. Forty years ago, no house could be seen from its windows. It was " in the country." But now, streets of houses are observable from every window, and the House is incongruous where once it was supreme. Speculative builders have their eyes on it. Its grounds, they say, would cut up very nicely into desirable building lots.

The morning-room, in which we are to meet throughout the play, seems to be aware of its impending doom, and the furniture, to have a dismal knowledge of dispersal soon to occur. The last of the Leppers, who believed in solidity, has gone to his grave, and in a little while the signs of the solidity in which he believed will go too. Such is the spirit a sensitive visitor might find brooding over the darkened room.

The door opens, and KATE, an elderly domestic servant, enters, followed by FANNY CAIRNS, Sir Samuel's niece, and her son, ARTHUR. KATE is about sixty, a woman with a benign and beautifully serene face. MRS. CAIRNS, whose age is forty-five, is a brisk, energetic and remarkably tenacious woman. She never has more than one idea in her head at a time, but she holds on to it like grim death. She is handsome in an efficient, charmless fashion. ARTHUR, her son, aged twenty-three, is a graduate of Oxford and excessively impressed by his own opinions. He shoots short sharp questions at you as if they were accusations of ineptitude and depravity. His mother is wearing *deeply black mourning garments, but* ARTHUR, *although his suit is dark, disdains these obsolete emblems of woe. His double-breasted navy-blue suit and his black shoes are the most that he will concede to bourgeois sentiment and middle-class convention. Suits of solemn black cannot denote* ARTHUR *truly, as he will inform any one who is incautious enough to listen to him. The past went into the grave at Dundonald this afternoon, and there, if* ARTHUR *has anything to say in the matter, it will remain.*

FANNY (*as she enters*). Oh, Kate, the blinds are still drawn !

KATE. Yes, mem. I didn't like to let them up till I was told. An' it wouldn't be like the thing to show the light too soon after a funer'l. It'd look as if you were in a hurry to get rid of the dead.

ARTHUR (*letting a blind up with a bang*). I hate all this gloom.

FANNY. Let them all up, Kate. The others will be here presently.

KATE (*as she releases the blinds and draws back the curtains from the French window which gives on to the garden*). It's quaren nice to see the sun again. Sir Sam had a great fancy for light.

ARTHUR. Why do we darken the house when people die?

KATE. It's the custom, sir. A house is always dark when people die, even if the blinds aren't drawn. God knows there's little we can do for the dead . . . except show them respect.

ARTHUR. Respect ! I don't call it respect to darken and depress the whole house. Let there be light—and plenty of it.

[*He opens the French window, and stands leaning against it, as he gazes into the garden.*]

KATE. M'yes, but it's the custom, sir. You could hardly go to a funer'l as if you were goin' to a trip.

ARTHUR. Supposing you don't respect the dead?

KATE (*deeply shocked*). Oh, but you must, sir. Everybody must respect the dead.

ARTHUR. Why?

KATE. I don't know, sir. I suppose it's because they're dead . . . an' defenceless.

ARTHUR (*almost snorting*). Huh! Mysticism!

KATE. I don't know that word, sir.

ARTHUR. It's better known as punk.

KATE (*giving him up*). You'll be makin' a lot of changes here, mem?

FANNY. Well that depends, Kate. I don't know yet that it's my house.

KATE. Oh, it'll be yours all right. Will there be many comin', do you think?

FANNY. Six or seven, probably. Mrs. Corken! . . .

KATE. Oh, ay, of course. She's very fond of funer'ls.

FANNY. And Mr. Finlay. Ourselves, of course! And my brother!

KATE. Ay. Well, I'd better just arrange these chairs round the table, so's you can all sit down in ease an' comfort.

[*She sets the chairs in position, placing one of them
conspicuously at the head of the table. It is for
MR. FINLAY. KATE has a strong sense of occasion.*]

ARTHUR (*coming away from the French window*). I hope the old boy's left me something.

KATE. Oh, I daresay he has. I daresay he's left you all something substantial. He had a great feelin' for his family.

FANNY. That isn't the way to speak of him, Arthur.

ARTHUR. What isn't?

FANNY. Old boy! He's hardly in his grave an hour yet!

ARTHUR. How long must he be there before I can speak about him naturally?

FANNY (*acidly*). That remark is neither clever nor funny: it's unmannerly.

KATE. Sir Sam won't mind, mem. He knows what boys are like.

ARTHUR. Boys!

KATE (*who has no sense of being insolent to her social superior*). Yes, sir.

ARTHUR. I wasn't trying to be funny, mother. Or clever, I was only asking for information.

FANNY. I daresay. But there's decency in everything.

KATE. Sometimes, sir, you ask people for information as if you were layin' a charge against them.

FANNY. I quite agree with you, Kate. That suit you're wearing, Arthur, is not my idea of mourning.

ARTHUR. No, but it's mine. I'm against this crepe-covered world-darkness and gloom and pumped-up despondency. 'Tis not alone my inky cloak, good mother, that can denote me truly.

FANNY. You have to have an undergraduate mind, Arthur, to be epigrammatic at a grave. One of these days, I hope, you'll become adult.

KATE. I think these chairs'll do nicely now.

FANNY. Yes, thank you, Kate. Nicely.

[*Her brother, EDWARD SCANTLEBURY, enters. His age is fifty-three, and he looks what he is: a soaker. His chief occupation is drinking. In his spare time, he plays golf . . . that is to say, after he has had a drink, he toddles round a course to make himself fit to have another drink. If there were no bars in Golf Clubs, he would give up golf and take to darts or billiards in a pub. He has a flabby paunch and watery blue eyes, and his hands occasionally tremble. There is almost always a smell of stale whiskey on his lips.*]

EDWARD (*who is cold*). Arrh! Booo! What about a drink, Kate?

KATE. Yes, sir.

FANNY. Can't you wait?

EDWARD. No. I'm perished. And my throat's like a lime-kiln. Where's the whiskey?

KATE. I'll just get it, sir.

FANNY. Bring the sherry, too, Kate.

KATE. It's the custom to have port, mem.

FANNY. Bring that as well.

KATE. Yes, mem.   [*Exit.*

EDWARD. Great old stand-by, Kate.

ARTHUR. I daresay the old boy's left her a good bit.

FANNY. Arthur!

ARTHUR. Oh, mother, I can't keep on remembering to respect the dead.

EDWARD. I hope he has left her a good bit. I hope he's left us all a good bit. You'll get a fine whack, Fanny. I shouldn't wonder if you get nearly the lot. This house, anyway.

FANNY. I haven't thought about it.

ARTHUR. Oh, mother, you've hardly thought of anything else for the last seven years.

EDWARD. Nor have I. It's been on my mind most of my life. I hope old Finlay'll hurry up. I hate suspense.

FANNY. I won't deny I have hopes of what Uncle Sam has left me, but I don't like the way Arthur talks about it. You should show respect, Arthur, even if you don't feel it.

ARTHUR. Why be hypocritical about it?

FANNY. Are you calling your mother a hypocrite?

ARTHUR. Well, not precisely! . . .

FANNY. Precisely or not precisely, you're insolent. If you can't respect the dead, at least respect the living.

EDWARD. Now, now, don't quarrel, you two. I hate rows, especially at funerals. Damned draughty, drouthy things in themselves, apart from rows. The wind blowing round that graveyard to-day was enough to cut the heart out of you.

FANNY. If you drank less, you wouldn't feel the cold.

EDWARD. It's because I feel the cold, I drink so much.

FANNY. I didn't notice any draught at the grave, and it's a beautiful sunny day.

EDWARD. My dear Fanny, it's a scientific fact that women don't feel the cold half as much as men do. That's why they're good at swimming. Their bodies are padded with fat! . . .

FANNY. Don't be disgusting.

EDWARD. A scientific fact is a scientific fact. There's nothing disgusting about it. Pers'nally, I'm here because I hope the old man's left me a good big dollop of dough. I need it, I can tell you. I'm up to my neck in debt. Mind you, I'm not going to be hypocritical about it. I didn't like Sir Sam. That's putting it mildly. I couldn't stand the old swipe! . . .

FANNY. Edward! Edward!

EDWARD. It's no use Edward-Edwarding me! If he can hear me, I hope he's listening hard. One of the comforting things about a hereafter is it enables people to learn the truth about themselves.

ARTHUR. In that case, the hereafter won't be much fun for you.

EDWARD. Who are you talking to, you pup? You're above yourself, my lad. Learn behaviour!

ARTHUR. There's nothing the matter with my behaviour.

EDWARD. Huh, isn't there? That's where you make your mistake. Let me tell you that. If you were to stop thinking you can think, you'd be intelligent. The biggest mistake you ever made was in being born!

FANNY. Quit it, will you? If you can't control your tongue, Arthur, go to your room and stay there. I suppose you're drunk, Edward.

EDWARD. Damn the drunk! I just spoke my mind, as this putty-faced brat of yours wanted, and all the thanks I get for my candour is abuse. Anyway, like it or not like it, I had no use whatever for Sir Sam. He was a selfish and tyrannical old devil. Put that in your pipe and smoke it. And if smoking's allowed where he is now, I hope he'll smoke it, too!

ARTHUR. You didn't like him much yourself, mother.

FANNY. I liked him as well as a poor relation can like a rich one.

EDWARD. He despised us, and he let us see he did. He had no natural affection. When I was in a mess two years ago, would he get me out of it? Not he! Not he! He told me to stew in my own juice if I had any juice to stew in. That was a nice way to talk to his own flesh and blood. All I asked him for was five hundred quid, and he wouldn't let me have it.

ARTHUR. Five hundred was a lot of money, uncle.

EDWARD. What! For a man that was a millionaire?

FANNY. Why should he let you sponge on him because he was rich.

EDWARD. Amn't I his own kith and kin? If a man can't support his relations, who can he support? You've done a bit of sponging on him yourself, my girl.

FANNY. How dare you say that?

EDWARD. I dare do all that man dare do. Don't think I'm afraid to open my mouth. He's kept you ever since

Willie died and left you without a ha'penny. (*He rounds on* ARTHUR.) *And* you. *And* your sister.

ARTHUR. Well, why not? With all that money, why shouldn't he keep us?

EDWARD. Och, I'm not saying anything against that. I didn't care how many he kept, as long as he kept me in the style I was accustomed to. That's not the argument. All I'm saying is that you haven't done so badly for yourselves, so why curse me? He sent you to Eton and Oxford, didn't he? That must 'a' set him back a good bit. And didn't he send Doreen to St. Leonards? It would 'a' been national schools for the pair of you, but for him. Well, why shouldn't he have stumped up five hundred for his only nephew. That's what I was, the only nephew he had in the wide world. And he refused me. (KATE *enters, carrying decanters and glasses on a tray*.) Oh, thank you, Kate. You've rescued the perishing. (*He takes the whiskey from her and pours out a large tot*.)

KATE. Soda, sir?

EDWARD. Och, no! Well, just a splash! (*He syphons a little of the soda into his glass*.)

KATE (*to Fanny*). I wonder, will there be enough here, mem?

FANNY. I should think so. Unless Mr. Edward! . . .

EDWARD. I'll ring if I want any more.

KATE. Very good, sir. (*She lays the tray on the table*.) There's a nice seed cake in the pantry, mem. Will I bring it in? It's the custom to have seed cake *and* wine at a funer'l.

EDWARD. Seed cake! The stuff people puts in their insides!

FANNY. No, thank you, Kate. People don't take refreshments at funerals now the way they used to.

KATE. No, mem, no. It was lunch one time, an' the table loadened, but now it's hardly tea. That's a pity. It's nice, I think, to have your friends and relations sittin' round the table, eatin' a meal in your memory. Very nice. But times have changed. Ay! Will I bring *you* somethin', mem?

FANNY. No, thank you.

KATE. Well, just ring if there's anythin' you want.

[DOREEN *enters, a pretty, good-natured, shallow girl of twenty or thereabouts. Her clothes are black.*]

DOREEN. Hillo, Kate!

KATE (*smiling affectionately at her*). Would you like me to bring you somethin', Miss Doreen?

DOREEN. Nothing, thanks. (*To her mother.*) When does it start?

FANNY (*irritably*). When does what start?

DOREEN. Reading the will, mother!

FANNY. As soon as Mr. Finlay arrives.

DOREEN. You ought to be at it, Kate. Uncle Sam's sure to have left you something.

KATE. Oh, no, Miss Doreen. That wouldn't be like the thing at all. Servants are never there when wills are read.

ARTHUR. Why not, if they're beneficiaries?

KATE. It's not the custom, sir.

ARTHUR. Funny how everybody gives you the same answer. It's not the custom! It's not the custom! . . .

KATE. Well, sir, it isn't. [*She goes out.*

ARTHUR. The working-classes are very conservative. The last fortress of feudalism is the peasant's cottage.

DOREEN (*deriding him*). Special note for the programme. The epigram in the second act was supplied by Mr. Arthur Scantlebury, the pride of Pembroke. (*To her mother.*) Who was that woman at the funeral?

FANNY. What woman? I didn't notice any woman.

EDWARD. Yes, I noticed her. Good-looking piece.

DOREEN. She behaved as if she were one of us.

ARTHUR. How do you mean—one of us?

DOREEN. You know—family.

FANNY. Nonsense, Doreen. Your head's full of fancies.

EDWARD. Well, I must say she seemed to be pushing herself forward. I mean, she wasn't just taking an interest in the thing.

FANNY. Lots of people go to funerals who have no right to be there. It's morbid curiosity, that's all.

[KATE *enters.*

KATE. Mr. Bothwell.

FANNY. Adam!

EDWARD. Now, what does he want here?

B

[ADAM BOTHWELL, *whose age is forty-nine, enters. His manner is diffident, as if he were uncertain of his reception, but his humorous and kind eyes denote greater strength of character than his diffidence might lead one to expect.*]

DOREEN. Hillo, Adam!

ADAM. I don't feel that I ought to be here, but Mr. Finlay told me to turn up. He said I might hear of something to my advantage.

DOREEN. Good! That means Uncle Sam's left you a legacy.

ADAM. I shall be greatly surprised if he has.

DOREEN. He may have left you all his money!

ADAM (*with a deprecating smile*). Oh, no! Oh, dear me, no! If I'm mentioned at all, it will be with contempt. Sir Sam disliked me! . . .

ARTHUR. Why?

ADAM. Perhaps *disliked* is too strong a term. It implies an interest in me that he never felt. Sir Sam ignored my existence. Probably he despised me! . . .

DOREEN. But you're not despicable, Adam.

ADAM. Oh, thank you, Doreen. That's very charming of you. *Despised,* perhaps, is also too strong a term. Isn't it odd what difficulty we have in finding the exact word to express our meaning? Sir Sam was a plain, blunt business man, with no frills about him, as he sometimes told me, and I'm a writer with rows and rows of frills. Naturally, he had no sympathy whatsoever with me, especially as I don't earn much by my work. He made a great deal of money by his own efforts! . . .

ARTHUR. I deny that. He exploited! . . .

FANNY. Keep that for the Oxford Union, Arthur.

ADAM. Well, anyhow, he made a great deal of money. He was a knight! . . .

ARTHUR. Knights are nothing!

ADAM. Are they? People still seem anxious to become knights.

EDWARD. Every time I go for a walk, I trip over a knight. You can hardly throw a stone in Belfast without hitting one.

FANNY. He had no cause to despise you.

DOREEN. You're quite well-known, Adam.

ADAM. Am I? By whom?

DOREEN. I met a man last summer who knew all about you.

ADAM (*delighted*). Did you? Really?

DOREEN. You remember, mother, that man we met at Torquay? He lectured on literature or something.

FANNY. Oh, yes, I remember. Funny-looking man with a beard. . . . Read a lot, but couldn't play bridge. He knew more about your books than I do, Adam.

ADAM (*dashed*). That wouldn't be difficult, Fanny. You don't know anything about them.

FANNY. Nonsense. I can't read them, but I *do* know about them.

EDWARD. Of course, your stuff's above my head, Adam. Artistic and all that, of course. But it hasn't got the . . . you know. (*Cracks his fingers in the air as if he were suggesting profundities.*) I don't pretend to be literary or anything like that, though I daresay I could write as well as most of those who do. It's a knack, you know, just a knack.

FANNY. Besides, Adam, you're an honorary LL.D. of Queen's.

ADAM. Uncle Sam thought little of degrees, earned or honorary. He had only one way of measuring a man's success. How much money had he made?

EDWARD. Well, it's as good a test as any. Come down to the bedrock of things, and what's the proof of any man's success. The power he possesses. And what's money but power. A man with a million is more powerful than a man with a *make*. Personally, I prefer breeding, but then everybody doesn't think as I think.

ADAM. I don't despise money. No, indeed! I like it. It brings all the things that make life agreeable . . . culture, travel, pleasant ways of living. Don't imagine that I have any Franciscan ideas about the blessedness of poverty. Those who have, usually possess ample private means. Poor people have no illusions about poverty. They know very well that it's one thing to go without boots because you like being barefooted, and another thing to go barefooted because you can't afford to buy boots.

DOREEN. Everybody praises your books, Adam.

ADAM. Yes, I'm what's called a critic's author. My reviews are good and my sales appalling. I have the largest following of people who don't read me of any author in the history of literature.

ARTHUR. That's a distinction in itself.

ADAM. Do you know, I've never been at the reading of a will before. What do we do? Sit around, listening to a solicitor reading out a long document in dreadful English? I might be able to use the scene in a novel.

FANNY. Is there nothing sacred to writers? How can you come here to make . . . copy out of a corpse.

ARTHUR. Why not? Why should the dead get off when the living don't?

FANNY. Exploiting the dead! Horrible!

ADAM. I'm sorry, Fanny. I was only joking! . . .

FANNY. Joking! That makes it worse. Don't any of you realize that Uncle Sam has just been buried? This isn't a time to be funny.

ADAM. You're quite right, Fanny. It was execrable taste.

EDWARD. The fool of the family used to go into the Navy. Now, he writes books.

DOREEN (*angrily*). I suppose you started life somewhere between the two periods, Uncle Edward?

EDWARD. Not funny, my girl, not funny! Just cheeky! What you two need, and what you never got, is a damned good skelping.

FANNY. Is there any need for all this rudeness? Doreen!

DOREEN. You've both been as rude to Adam as you can, and when I'm rude back, you tick me off. What's sauce for Adam should be sauce for a couple of ganders.

FANNY. That's enough! I don't want to hear any more.

ARTHUR. Why not?

EDWARD. Can't you say anything but " why not "? Hundreds of pounds have been spent on your education, but you've got the most limited vocabulary of any man I know. Why not? Why not? Why not? This country's over-run by people that ask questions, but don't listen to answers.

DOREEN. Arthur knows the answers to all the questions, don't you, Arthur?

ARTHUR. I don't want any lip from a flapper.

EDWARD. What the hell's keeping this fellow, Finlay? Have a drink, Adam?

ADAM. No, thanks, I don't drink.

EDWARD. Don't drink? What do you do? (*Helping himself to one.*)

ADAM. Oh, a few things.

EDWARD. Anybody else like a drink?

FANNY. No, and I think you've had enough. If you go on like this, you'll be drunk before the will's read.

EDWARD. Drunk! Me? I could drain a distillery and not notice it. Well, here's mud in your eye! (*Takes a swig.*) Gosh, that's done me good! Standing about in draughty graveyards makes me damned dry. Ah, drink's the curse of Ireland. It is, indeed. If it isn't whiskey, it's porter, and if it isn't porter, it's tea, an' sure, tea's the worst of the lot. The tea drunkards of Ireland, poor souls!

ARTHUR. How much do you think the old boy's left?

EDWARD. God knows. And Finlay, of course. As near a million as makes no differs. Of course, there'll be the death duties. That's robbery, if you like.

ARTHUR. It's terrible to think of one man having all that money.

EDWARD. What's terrible about it?

DOREEN. He made it, didn't he?

ARTHUR. And how? How? I ask you. By exploiting the proletariat!

ADAM. Must you call decent workmen by that disgusting name?

ARTHUR. Bah! Bourgeois cant and humbug! Romantic nonsense about individual effort. There's no such thing! All effort is communal. Everything that a man does is founded on the work of other people! We're in everybody's debt! . . .

DOREEN (*intoning like a church chime*). Blah, blah, blah, blah, blah, blah, blah, blah! This is the Northern Ireland station speaking. Comrade Arthur Cairns, the well-known authority on everything, will now explain the meaning of the universe. Comrade Arthur Cairns! . . .

EDWARD. You're a dilletante Communist, Arthur. That's what you are. A dilletante Communist.

DOREEN. He's gone native, Uncle Edward. He's a Nationalist, now, and thinks De Valera is God's little boy!

EDWARD. Well, whatever he is, he won't refuse any of Sir Sam's rhino.

ARTHUR. I shall put it to a good use. Destroy the enemy with his own weapons.

EDWARD. Undergraduates have a strange effect on me. They make me want to puke. Wherever in this world there's a damned silly row going on, students are in it up to their necks.

ARTHUR. Go on. Belittle the young! That's all the old can do!

ADAM. How often I've heard that remark. It's made every twenty-five years, and those who make it to-day, resent it to-morrow.

[MRS. CORKEN *enters. She is a heavily-built, sluggish woman, in whose eyes, however, if you look closely enough, you will see signs of a malicious leer. Her age is seventy, and she's a bit of a rip. Her mourning is deep: she's almost smothered in crape. The exertion of entering the house has tired her, and she is panting.*]

FANNY (*going to greet her*). Oh, Aunt Essie! Didn't Kate show you in?

MRS. CORKEN (*after waving her hand as if she were demanding patience while she recovers her breath*). I . . . I . . . don't need anybody . . . to show me . . . into this . . . house. Oh, dear, I'm all out of puff!

FANNY (*pushing a chair towards her*). Sit down, dear. (MRS. CORKEN *does so*.) You shouldn't have come. We'd have told you! . . .

MRS. CORKEN (*ignoring her niece*). Oh, dear. Oh, dear. Oh, dear! (*Then in a drawn-out relieved way*.) Ohhhhh, dear!

EDWARD. Feel better now?

MRS. CORKEN. Ay, ay!

EDWARD. Like a drink or anything?

MRS. CORKEN. Ah, don't bother me with your drink! In a previous existence, Edward, you must have been a vat.

EDWARD. I wish I was one now.

MRS. CORKEN. Is that you, Adam? How are you?

ADAM. I have my health, as Kate would say.

MRS. CORKEN. Och, dear, oh dear, oh dear! Ech-ech!
. . . Well, this is a sad day, a *sad* day!

EDWARD. Ah, sure, we'll all have to come to it. Somebody said death's the great democrat, but it's more like a
dictator.

FANNY. You know, you're not fit for this sort of thing,
Aunt Essie. You tire yourself out! . . .

MRS. CORKEN. I've never missed a family funer'l in
my life, and I'm not going to start missing one now, not
when it's my own brother's. I must say it was a grand
turn out.

FANNY. Yes, it was. Everybody was there.

EDWARD. Well, of course, say what you like about him,
Uncle Sam was an important man. It was only right and
natural that the Lord Mayor and Corporation should 'a'
been there, but I was gratified to see the Bishop and the
Dean. Considering that we're Presbyterians, that was very
nice of them.

ADAM. There are no sectarian differences in death.

MRS. CORKEN. I sincerely hope there are. It would be
a poor reward for maintaining your faith on earth, to find
it didn't matter in heaven.

DOREEN. Uncle Sam would 'a' been gratified if he could
'a' seen the crowd at his funeral.

MRS. CORKEN. How do you know he didn't. If I'm any
judge of character, Sam saw the whole outfit from start to
finish, and I'll take my Bible oath he noted down the names
of them that ought to 'a' been there, and weren't. I made
up my mind the minute I heard he was dead that nothing
short of a paralytic stroke would keep me away. I wasn't
going to have him casting it up to me on the Judgment
Day that I wasn't there, after him keeping me all these
years.

ADAM. But don't you think, now that he has acquired
what we hope is a larger view of things, he'd have made
allowances for you if you'd stayed at home.

MRS. CORKEN. Sam never made allowances for nobody
in his life, and he's not going to start making them now
he's dead. Is Mr. Finlay not here yet?

FANNY. We're expecting him every minute.

MRS. CORKEN. Well, Edward, at the drink again, I see.

EDWARD. No! No! No! Not what you'd call *at* it! Just standing by. That graveyard at Dundonald's a very draughty place. I think I got a wee bit of a chill on my liver.

MRS. CORKEN. What you've got on your liver is liquor. If ever you're dissected, Edward! . . .

EDWARD (*hurriedly drinking*). For God's sake, Aunt Essie!

MRS. CORKEN. The doctor'll find a liver like the Rock of Gibraltar! Ah, dear, dear, dear! these are trying times. People dying every day. I don't like the way things are going on at all. There seems to be more deaths now than ever there was.

ARTHUR. No, aunt, you're wrong. The death-rate is dropping.

MRS. CORKEN. Is it, indeed? Well, I never lift the *News-Letter* or the *Telegraph* without seeing a string of deaths, and half of them mebbe people I know. You're getting a fine girl, Doreen. Come here 'til I have a look at you. (DOREEN *approaches the old lady*.) Ay, you're getting a fine lump of a girl. You used to be a long-legged, skinny looking thing, but you're filling out. You'll be losing her before long, Fanny.

DOREEN. Oh, auntie, I'm very healthy.

MRS. CORKEN. Och, I don't mean that kind of loss, dear. Some young fellow'll come along and lift you off your feet!

FANNY. Time enough for that!

MRS. CORKEN. Oh, no, a girl can't get married too soon. I've known a few get married too late. If Sam's left Doreen a substantial sum, the boys'll be buzzing round her like a bumble bee round a jam jar. What brings you here, Adam?

ADAM. Curiosity, I suppose, but a sort of family feeling, too. A death seems to draw relations together. I've just been saying that Sir Sam didn't like me much.

MRS. CORKEN. It was those books you write. Poor things that just go doddering on from page to page. It never seems to me to matter where you start them or where you stop. They read as well backways as frontways. I mind Sam saying to me one day, " Essie," says he, " how in the name of God did we come to have an author in the family?" and I said, " Sam," I said, " I can't imagine. There's never been the like of that in our family before! "

ADAM. But I don't do any harm, Aunt Essie.

MRS. CORKEN. Do you do any good?

ADAM. Well, I don't interfere with people. So long as I'm allowed to do what I like, they can do whatever they like.

FANNY. I should have thought you'd want to be a good influence Adam.

ADAM. No—no, I don't. I've seen a great deal of misery caused by people who wanted to be a good influence. I'm content to leave people alone.

ARTHUR. Pah! What an ambition! You're no better than a limpet, clinging to a rock.

ADAM. Well, so long as there's a rock to cling to, that's all right.

[KATE opens the door and announces the family solicitor.]

KATE. Mr. Finlay!

MRS. CORKEN. And about time, too.

[JAMES FINLAY enters . . . a busy-looking man, about sixty, very neat, without being noticeable or dapper. His manner is sharp and decided, and his speech terse. He carries a despatch-case.]

FINLAY. I'm late! . . .

MRS. CORKEN. Heth, you are! Sam won't like it.

FINLAY. I was kept. Very remarkable funeral, Mrs. Cairns. I've seldom seen so many people round a grave.

MRS. CORKEN. There's always been a crowd at a funeral in our family. When my husband died . . . let me see, how long ago was that?

FINLAY. Twenty-five years ago, nearly to the tick.

MRS. CORKEN. Is it all that while? What an elapse of time!

FINLAY. Is any one else coming?

FANNY. No.

FINLAY. Then as I've got to get back to town very soon,

I'll just tell you briefly the terms of the will. I won't read the will itself. It's a long document, and legal language isn't easy to follow if you're not used to it. In any case, I have a letter to read to you! . . .

Mrs. Corken. Letter! Who from?

Finlay. Your brother, Mrs. Corken.

Fanny. Uncle Sam!

Finlay. Yes. After he had signed his will, he handed me a sealed letter and instructed me to read it to you before opening the will. I know what's in the will, but I don't know what's in this letter.

Mrs. Corken. It sounds fearful to get a letter from a dead man. I don't like it.

Arthur. The will itself's a letter from the dead, aunt.

Mrs. Corken. Och, it's not the same thing at all. A will's in a lawyer's hand, but this letter'll be in Sam's. I don't like it at all.

Finlay. I'm obliged to read it to you, Mrs. Corken. Sir Samuel's instructions were definite and detailed. They're in the will itself.

Mrs. Corken. Oh, all right, then, but don't any of you be surprised if I go off in a dead faint.

Finlay. I daresay we'll be able to bring you round in time to hear the bequests. Will you please all seat yourselves and I'll read the letter.

[*He takes the head of the table, laying his despatch-case in front of him. Mrs. Corken remains in an arm-chair at the side of the room. Fanny seats herself at Finlay's right, Edward on his left. Beside Edward sits Doreen, and next to her Arthur. Adam seats himself at the foot of the table. He has a vacant chair beside him. Finlay opens his despatch-case, and takes out the letter and the will.*]

Finlay. This is the Last Will and Testament of Sir Samuel Lepper, deceased. And this is a sealed letter which he directed me to read to you before I opened the will. I'd like you all to look at the letter, to see that it is properly sealed and that it bears Sir Samuel's handwriting on the envelope. I wish you to understand that I do not know, any more than you do, what's in the letter. Will you take a look at it, Mrs. Corken?

[*He offers it to her, but she waves it away.*

MRS. CORKEN. I'll take your word for it.

FINLAY (*handing the letter to* FANNY). Pass it round, please, after you've examined it.

FANNY. It looks all right to me.

[*The letter is passed from hand to hand, and is eventually returned to* FINLAY. *While it is being circulated,* EDWARD *delivers himself of a few remarks.*]

EDWARD. This is very irregular, Mr. Finlay.

FINLAY. Irregular?

EDWARD. Ay. The will ought to be enough. We don't want any correspondence about it.

FINLAY. Sir Samuel wanted to have a quiet talk with you all! . . .

MRS. CORKEN. Talk? What do you mean by *talk?*

FINLAY. In a manner of speaking. He didn't want anybody but yourselves to hear him. If he'd put his remarks in his will, the world could read them. You see, Mrs. Corken, a will's a public document, and has to be filed in a public office, where anybody can have a look at it for a shilling or get a copy of it for three-and-six.

MRS. CORKEN. Dear-oh-dear, can a body not die in private now?

FINLAY. He cannot. Dying gets more and more public every day. You can nearly listen in to a man dying these times.

MRS. CORKEN. All your affairs broadcast to the wide world. What'll be the end of it all. No place in the world where a body can be by himself! . . .

[*By this time, the letter has been returned to the solicitor.*]

FINLAY. Are you satisfied that this letter is properly sealed, and that it bears the handwriting on its envelope of the late Sir Samuel Lepper?

FANNY. We are.

[*Murmurs of agreement from the rest.*

FINLAY. Then I'll open it and read it aloud.

[*Before he can do so,* KATE *opens the door and enters.*]

KATE. There's a woman outside wants to come in.

FANNY. What woman?

KATE. I don't know.

EDWARD (*irritably*). Well, what does she want?

KATE. She wants to come in.

FANNY. Didn't you tell her we're busy?

KATE. I did, but she said she had a right to be here.

EDWARD. Right! Right!

MRS. CORKEN. What right?

[JENNY CONN *enters. She is a trim, tolerably good-looking girl, with nice legs and an air of assurance. Her eyes are quick in observation, good, steady eyes that can stare back resolutely, and relax at once in laughter: a firm-willed woman, but not hard, not mulishly obdurate. Her age is about thirty, and she is a good companion and a trusty friend. She walks into the room as if it were her own.*]

FANNY (*who has risen in a fury*). How dare you come into this room? Who are you?

DOREEN. It's the girl I saw in the graveyard, mother.

JENNY (*to* ADAM). Move over a bit! (*He takes the next chair.*) I've more right to be here than any of you. (*She seats herself in* ADAM'S *chair.*)

FINLAY. This is a private family meeting! . . .

JENNY. I'm part of the family. Are you Mr. Finlay?

FINLAY. Yes.

JENNY. Then you'll know my name. I'm Jenny Conn! . . .

FINLAY (*disconcerted*). Oh, yes. M'yes!

FANNY. Do you know this woman, Mr. Finlay?

FINLAY. This is the first time I've ever laid eyes on her, but I . . . I know about her.

FANNY. Who is she?

EDWARD. Yes, who are you?

JENNY. Sir Sam's daughter.

MRS. CORKEN. What do you mean, girl? He hadn't got a daughter.

JENNY. Oh, yes, he had. I'm her.

FANNY. Do you say you're my uncle's daughter?

JENNY. Yes. Illegitimate.

MRS. CORKEN. My God Almighty!

JENNY (*taking a packet of papers out of her bag and laying them on the table*). If you don't believe me, read those. Mr. Finlay knows who I am.

DOREEN. You were at the funeral.

JENNY. I was. Why wouldn't I be at my father's funeral?

FANNY. I don't believe a word of it . . . not a word of it.

JENNY (*indicating the packet*). The proofs are there! My birth certificate and the letters that passed between my father and mother before and after I was born. And there's a photograph of them, taken when they were at Portrush together, about nine months before I was born. That was while his wife was alive.

MRS. CORKEN. Scandalous! Scandalous!

FANNY. Even if you are Sir Samuel's daughter! . . .

JENNY. I'm his daughter all right. Look at me! I'm the image of him.

MRS. CORKEN (*muttering to herself*). Bold as brass! Brazen! That's what you are. Brazen!

JENNY. You can all see I feature him.

ADAM. Yes, you're very like him.

EDWARD. That might be an accident.

JENNY. Heth, there was no accident about it. Not on my mother's side, anyhow. (*To Adam.*) Who are you?

ADAM. I'm Adam Bothwell . . . a distant relation of yours. How do you do? (*He shakes hands with her.*)

JENNY (*more genially or shall we say less aggressively*). I'm rightly, thank you.

FANNY. Even if you are his daughter, you've no right to be here. You say yourself, you're . . . illegitimate!

FINLAY. She may be mentioned in this letter, Mrs. Cairns.

FANNY (*subsiding*). Oh, yes. Yes, of course.

JENNY. You're Fanny, aren't you?

FANNY. I'm Mrs. Cairns.

JENNY. Are those your two children?

DOREEN. Yes. I'm Doreen. This is my brother, Arthur. If there's anything you want to know, he'll tell you.

JENNY (*to* EDWARD). I know who *you* are. Your breath can be smelt a mile away.

EDWARD. I'll thank you, young woman, to hold a civil tongue in your head. How do we know she's Sir Sam's daughter? We've only her word for it.

FANNY. Yes. These documents don't prove that she's the child mentioned in them.

JENNY. Look at me, Fanny. Look at me! (FANNY *does so*.) Do you doubt I'm his daughter?

[FANNY *does not answer, but averts her eyes. There is silence for a few moments.*]

FINLAY. Well?

ADAM. I think she should stay.

DOREEN. So do I.

ARTHUR. This is a slice of life, if you like. There's a theme for you here, Adam!

DOREEN. Mr. Bothwell writes books. Mebbe, you've read some.

JENNY. No, I can't say I have.

FINLAY. I take it, then, you've no objection, any of you, to Miss Conn remaining.

MRS. CORKEN. I have, but what's the use?

EDWARD. So have I. But as you say, what's the use?

FINLAY. Very well. Miss Conn! . . .

JENNY. I ought to be Lepper. I'm near in the mind to change it.

MRS. CORKEN. You'll take no such liberty.

JENNY. I've a better right to the name than any person in this room. I'm his daughter, and some of you are scarcely blood relations.

MRS. CORKEN. I'm his sister . . . the closest relative he had left.

JENNY. No, you're not. I am. A pretty penny you cost him . . . you and that man of yours. You lived on him.

MRS. CORKEN. How dare you, you terge! . . .

JENNY. It's no use losing your temper with me, Aunt Essie.

MRS. CORKEN (*almost dumbfounded*). Aunt *what!*

JENNY. That's what you are, aren't you? My Aunt Essie! Uncle Andy was a waster! . . .

MRS. CORKEN. God forbid I should lift my hand to you, girl!

JENNY. The two of you sponged on my father! . . .

MRS. CORKEN. Quit calling him your father.

JENNY. What else can I call him? He *was* my father, wasn't he? Uncle Andy never earned a penny-piece in his born days. He lived on his parents 'til he bankrupted them, and then he lived on my father 'til he died. That was the only time Uncle Andy saved any money! . . .

MRS. CORKEN. He was a fine man, a very fine man, with high ideals and noble aspirations. It wasn't his fault he lived in a world that didn't appreciate him. He was always and ever the first to tell anybody what to do. Time and again I heard him say, " If only people would listen to me, there'd be less trouble and distress! " But, sure, nobody ever did listen to him . . . except me, and what could I do? It would be a terrible blow to him to hear this news about Sam, as God-fearing a man, to outward appearance, as ever walked the earth. But, as the Bible says, men were deceivers ever.

ARTHUR. That isn't in the Bible. It's in Shakespeare.

MRS. CORKEN. It's true all the same. To think my brother, and him well-reared, should get a child in sin.

JENNY. There's very little difference, Aunt Essie, between a child that's got in sin and a child that's not. You couldn't tell the one from the other, if you didn't know.

FINLAY. Miss Conn, I'm about to read a letter left by your father. I don't know what it contains. He handed it to me, sealed as you see, with instructions to read it to his relations immediately after his burial and before opening his will. I was just about to do so when you came into the room. I'll read it now, if you please. (*There is silence while he breaks the seal and takes the letter out of the envelope. He flattens it on the table, and then, after he has placed his spectacles on his face, takes it up and reads it aloud.*) This is what he says :

" I am leaving this letter to be read to you by my Solicitor after I'm dead, because I hadn't the nerve to say what's in it to your faces. There's a belief that I'm a man with a strong sense of family, but the fact is, I've hardly any, and I've long been sick of the lot of you. There's scarcely one of you that hasn't sponged on me for years. Every time I opened my front door, I fell over a relation, wanting something. Yet none of you, so far as I'm aware, has the slightest affection for me or would have taken the trouble to visit me if I'd been a poor man."

DOREEN. Oh, that isn't true. I liked him.

FANNY. Do you think we should go on with this, Mr. Finlay?

FINLAY. I'm bound to go on with it, Mrs. Cairns. My instructions were clear and precise. But, of course, I can't compel you to stay and listen to it. Does any one wish to go.

MRS. CORKEN. To think of him cherishing all that ill will against his own flesh and blood.

ADAM. Go on, Mr. Finlay. Let's hear the worst.

FINLAY. Very well. (*Reading.*) "It is, I suppose, my own fault that I've never had affection from you. I never gave you any. But then I've never felt under an obligation to like people merely because they were related to me. You may wonder why, feeling as I do, I put up with you so long, and, indeed, I wonder myself; but I got a foolish pleasure out of the very thing I despised : it gratified me to hear people praising my family feeling and my generosity to my friends and relations, though there isn't one of you, barring Doreen and that odd fellow, Adam Bothwell, I care a single solitary damn about ! . . .

DOREEN (*suddenly in tears*). Oh, poor Uncle Sam !

FANNY. Doreen ! *Doreen!*

DOREEN. I can't bear to think he hated us all.

[JENNY *goes to her and puts her arm round her.*

JENNY. He didn't hate you. (*To* ARTHUR, *indicating the seat she has just left.*) Move over there, you !

ARTHUR. Why?

JENNY. Because I tell you. (ARTHUR, *giving her a look, as they say, changes his seat.* JENNY *takes his, her arm still round* DOREEN.) There, girl, there ! You've nothing to bring against yourself. He liked you, anyway. Keep your heart up. I'm sorry, Mr. Finlay. Go on.

FINLAY. If the young lady's distressed ! . . .

DOREEN. It's all right. I can bear it if Jenny sits beside me.

FINLAY (*reading*). "My sister, Esther Corken, and her husband would have drained me dry if I'd let them."

MRS. CORKEN. May God in His goodness forgive him for that. I don't know what Sam's saying to the Almighty this minute, but I hope he's begging His pardon. And if he meets my Andy, I hope he'll beg his, too.

FINLAY (*reading*). "I can't remember a time of my life, since their marriage, when I wasn't keeping that pair. Yet I never liked either of them. That's as true as I'm sitting in this chair, writing this letter. I never liked Essie any time. As a child, I couldn't thole her! . . .

MRS. CORKEN (*starting up*). I can't stay here and listen to this. Tell me what he's left me and let me go home.

FINLAY. He hasn't left you anything!

[*There is general dismay at this statement.*

MRS. CORKEN. What! Nothing! And me his own sister!

FINLAY. You'd better hear the whole letter, Mrs. Corken.

JENNY. Sure, these ones have heard what he said about you, Aunt Essie, and you'd better stay and hear what he has to say about them.

MRS. CORKEN. Don't you Aunt Essie me!

JENNY. That's all right.

MRS. CORKEN. Is there any more about me?

FINLAY. Yes, a bit more.

MRS. CORKEN. Oh, very well, go on. But if I ever meet Sam in the next world, I'll give him the queer look.

FINLAY (*reading*). "Andy Corken was a faluther of a fellow. He had the tongue of a tornado and the brains of a hen. I kept that man for seventeen solid years, the time he was married to Esther, and I've kept her ever since, and neither of them was worth their keep. Andy behaved as if he were a man of culture and charm, and I was an uncouth and almost illiterate merchant who had had the luck to make a fortune. I never detected a sign in him that I was his superior in every respect. He went to his grave deep in my debt, and took it as his due. I had nothing in common with Esther! . . ."

MRS. CORKEN. We had the same blood!

FINLAY. "There are bare acquaintances I liked better. But her line was that a man has a duty to maintain his

C

relations, whether he likes them or not. There are scores
of people, not related to me at all, that I like far better
than my kith and kin. Only I haven't the nerve to say so.
I let myself be imposed upon by people I despised, and I
get a silly pleasure out of seeing them sucking up to me,
and hearing myself admired for my goodness and my
generosity when I long to see them all selling matches in
the street. May God forgive me for being a hypocrite!
There's my nephew Edward Scantlebury! . . ." (EDWARD
braces himself for his ordeal) " . . . my second sister's son
—if there is anywhere on earth a more contemptible
specimen of humanity than Edward, I don't want to see
him."

EDWARD. If I'd known he thought like that about me,
I wouldn't 'a' touched a penny of his money.

JENNY. Oh, yes, you would. With that thirst of yours,
he could 'a' kicked you from here to Cork, an' you'd 'a'
taken all he gave you. He could 'a' wiped his boots on
your face, and you'd still have taken his money.

FINLAY. Please, please! (*Reads.*) "He is the laziest
and drunkenest man in Ireland, and God knows that's
saying a lot. Never in his life has that man done a decent
day's work. This would be a sweeter world, if he were
blotted off the earth! . . ."

EDWARD. I could take an action against him for that!

FINLAY. You can't sue the dead.

EDWARD. I suppose he knew that, the coward! Waited
'til he was dead and buried before he dared say what he
thought. What a man! What a man!

JENNY. A good man to live on, Old Soak!

EDWARD. Don't talk to me. I want no conversation
with you, Miss Whateveryournameis!

JENNY. That'll suit me rightly.

FINLAY (*reading*). "If the Almighty God had any reason
for making Edward, he must long ago have rued it. I let
this sot and sponger live on me because I hadn't the moral
courage to tell him to go to hell. The result is I've ruined
him. Take a look at him. That's what I did to him with
my good nature and my strong sense of family. I'm near
in the mind, Edward, to beg your pardon for making a
worthless waster of you." That's all he has to say about
you, Scantlebury.

EDWARD. It's plenty. What's he left me?

FINLAY. Nothing.

EDWARD. My God. First he ruins me. Next he insults me. And then he leaves me penniless. I hope he's in hell.

FINLAY. The next part of the letter refers to you, Mrs. Cairns, and your children. (*Reading.*) " Then there's my niece, Fanny, and her two children. I have great respect for Fanny, but no liking. She knows what she wants, and she does her best to get it. She's as tough as I am, tougher, for she hasn't a hap'porth of sentimentality in her whole composition, and I respect her for it. She thinks of nothing but her own and her children's interest, as if their welfare was more important than that of any other living creature. Every prayer she utters is for her and them. I said to her once, ' Do you think God'll favour your family more than another because you try to bribe Him with a prayer or two? ' and she could hardly answer me, she was in such a rage. Yes, Fanny, you're a tough woman and I like tough women. You were determined to make me keep you and your children, and I kept them. You made up your mind that they should have the best I could afford, and they had it. I sent Arthur to Eton and Oxford, and ruined the snipe! . . . "

ARTHUR. The what?

FINLAY. Snipe! (*Reading.*) " He now spends his time denouncing his elders, though he lives on their means. He's a perfect example of an educated ass, and I hope he'll become a schoolmaster. That'll serve him right, though it'll be hard on the boys he has to teach. I'm fond of Doreen. She'd be all right if her mother would leave her alone. But Fanny will never leave any one alone. Will you, Fanny? "

FANNY (*startled*). What's that?

FINLAY. It's part of the letter, Mrs. Cairns.

FANNY. Oh! Oh, yes!

FINLAY (*reading*). " She must interfere with other people. If she finds you sitting in one chair, she asks you if you wouldn't be more comfortable in another. She's always peeping at you, watching you, telling you. Her son's always telling you, too, but the difference between him and her is, she has something to tell you, and he hasn't. She has a will of her own, and I like that, though I can't say I like her. It's agitated my mind a great deal to know what to do about her. If I leave her to her own resources, she'll develop her wits and maybe make something worth while of herself and her children, but if I leave her a fortune, she'll degenerate into something like Esther! . . . "

MRS. CORKEN. Can't he leave me alone?

FINLAY (*reading*). "Doreen is a girl that likes an easy life. I doubt if a hard life would do her any good. It might do her a lot of harm. She hasn't enough strength of character to stick out for herself. She'll go where she's led. I don't hold that against her. I merely mention it as a fact. She needs protection. Given that, she'll do well enough. Arthur won't do at all. I've never heard that fellow praise anything. I know what he hates, but I don't know what he likes. If he does manage to say a good word for anybody, he does it by running some other person down. These three are a trouble to me. Fanny's absolutely certain she has a right to a front seat at everything, though she's never done a hand's turn to deserve it. That's cheek, of course, but it is also courage, and I like courage, even when it's foolish! . . . "

ARTHUR (*impatiently*). What's he left us?

FINLAY. Nothing.

FANNY & ARTHUR (*standing up in their astonishment*). Nothing!

FINLAY. Not a ha'penny . . . to you. He's left a thousand pounds to Doreen.

MRS. CORKEN. That won't carry her far, with her tastes.

JENNY (*to* DOREEN). It'll keep you while you're learning a job.

DOREEN. I don't want a job.

FINLAY. I'm coming to the end now. (*Reading.*) "My second cousin, Adam Bothwell, is the only member of my family that's never bothered me for anything, but I don't know whether that's because he has too much spirit to sponge on me or not enough to try it on. I haven't anything against him, except the books he writes. I bought them all as they came out, partly to help the fellow a bit, but more to find out what his mind was up to, but I was never able to finish any of them, and some I couldn't start. He's a harmless, poor creature, with no wish to get in any person's way. I suppose that's as good a way of living as any."

JENNY. He's let you off light.

ADAM. Is that what you call light?

FINLAY. Please. (*Reading.*) "Well, that's all I have to say about you, friends and relations. I can't say it would have been any loss if I'd never seen one of you. I'd be a lot better off if I hadn't. There's a man in the Bible I've often envied : Melchisidec, that had no relations of any shape or size. I'd like to resemble him, to be destitute of every kind of tie, no kindred, no home, no country, nothing that binds me to any mortal thing. I read one time in a book that the Desert Fathers spurned their families and rejoiced when they heard of a relation's death. One tie the less to bind them to this earth. That's what I've always wanted—to be absolutely free. But I've never had enough strength or character for that; or I was too vain. I was only fit to be rich and surrounded by sycophants and spongers. That's the punishment every rich man receives. It's his hell on earth, and you've all been mine. I feel I've done you enough harm by maintaining you when I'd have done better to let you earn your own living, and I can't go comfortably to my grave with the thought in my head that I'm completing your ruin by leaving you all I have. It's taken me a long time to come to this decision, but I've come to it. I've left five hundred pounds, and an annuity of three pounds a week to Kate, and I hope she'll live long to enjoy it ! . . ."

DOREEN. Oh, I'm glad he left her something.

FINLAY (*reading*). "And I'd like here to thank her for the way she has always worked for me. God bless you, Kate."

DOREEN. Let's bring her in and tell her what he said about her.

[*She starts towards the door as she speaks, but her mother forbids her.*]

FANNY. Sit down, Doreen, and don't be silly. Kate will learn soon enough. (*Turning to* FINLAY.) What happens to the money?

JENNY. Does he mention me at all?

FINLAY (*glancing at the end of the letter*). Yes, but oddly . . . in a postscript.

JENNY. A postscript!

FANNY. What happens to the money?

FINLAY (*reading*). " I have decided, after long and deep consideration, to leave the whole of my fortune to my second cousin, Adam Bothwell! . . . "

FANNY. Adam!

MRS. CORKEN. You!

EDWARD. Adam Bothwell!

ADAM. Me!

FINLAY. Yes.

ADAM. But that can't be right. He didn't like me! . . .

ARTHUR. He didn't like any of us.

ADAM. But he particularly didn't like me. The last time we met—it must have been two years ago—he took one look at me and said, " So you're still about? " I felt I ought to give myself up to the police for being alive.

FINLAY. No, there's no mistake. I know, of course, because it's in the will. Apart from a few bequests for servants, including Kate, and a thousand pounds for Doreen, the whole fortune is yours.

ADAM. But I don't want all that money!

EDWARD. You can refuse it, then.

ARTHUR. Or take it and give it to us.

JENNY. How much is it?

FINLAY. I can't tell you yet. The Death Duties will be heavy, but, by and large, I'd say nearly half a million.

ADAM (*rising in a bewildered way*). But why me? He may have despised me, but what did I ever do to him that he should treat me like this? I never did him any harm! . . .

MRS. CORKEN. Well, you won't need to write any more books.

ADAM. But that's all I want to do. I don't want any man's money.

JENNY. Sit down and take a hold of yourself. (*He looks at her for a moment, and then subsides into his seat*). Are there any conditions, Mr. Finlay?

FINLAY. No, none. It's your money, Mr. Bothwell, to do what you like with.

JENNY. What did my father say about me?

FINLAY (*reading*). " I have an illegitimate daughter, Jenny Conn, who has greatly annoyed me all her life by refusing to let me do for her what I've done for the rest of my family. This is an inconsistency on my part. I admire the girl's independent spirit. She's my daughter all right. But I wanted badly to bring her up my way, not hers, and she wouldn't let me. She's right, of course, though that doesn't reconcile me to her behaviour. I've been tempted to leave my fortune to her, but my conscience forbids me to destroy her spirit. The girl is standing on her own feet, and I'd do her an injury if I tried to make her stand on mine. She has all she needs! . . . "

JENNY. Nobody has that.

FINLAY (*ignoring the interruption*). " . . . and, anyway, she's earning her own living. I don't want to demoralize her by taking her away from her work. There are enough parasites in this family already. I leave her to Adam Bothwell to deal with as he thinks fit." That's all, Miss Conn.

JENNY. And enough, too. (*Turning to Adam.*) How do you mean to deal with me, Adam?

ADAM. How am I going to deal with myself?

FINLAY. The will's here, if any of you wish to see it, but I can assure you that there's nothing in it that you don't already know.

DOREEN. We ought to tell Kate.

FANNY. Hold your tongue, Doreen.

DOREEN. I won't hold my tongue. I *will* tell her. (*She goes out*).

ARTHUR. Mutiny number one.

FINLAY. I'll be getting along. (*To* ADAM.) There are a number of details to be settled, Mr. Bothwell, but I'll get them fixed as soon as possible.

EDWARD (*at the whiskey bottle again*). You'll have a spot before you go, Finlay? Oh, I'm sorry, Adam. It's yours, of course.

ADAM. Never mind. Help yourself.

EDWARD. Well, thanks, I will. I've had a great shock.

[*Helps himself to a stiff one.*

MRS. CORKEN. It's a wicked will, Mr. Finlay, a wicked, wicked will! You should 'a' stopped him making it.

FINLAY. Sir Sam wasn't an easy man to stop, Mrs. Corken. (*Shaking hands with her.*) Good-bye!

MRS. CORKEN (*indifferently*). Oh, good-bye, good-bye!

ARTHUR. I suppose the will's all right. Can't it be upset?

EDWARD. Listen to the wee Bolshie!

FINLAY. No one has ever upset a will I've drawn up, Arthur, and I wouldn't advise you to try to upset this one. Good-day to you all. (*They murmur in reply, and he goes towards the door.*)

JENNY (*to* ADAM). See him out. It's your house now.

ADAM. Me?

JENNY. Yes. Assert yourself.

ADAM (*to* FINLAY). I'll just come to the door with you! . . .

FINLAY. Oh, there's no need! . . .

[*But they drift out together.*

EDWARD. My Jesus!

MRS. CORKEN. What's to become of us all? What'll I do?

EDWARD. Not a ha'penny! Not a damned ha'penny. And me up to my neck in debt. It's the Poorhouse for us. (*Seeing* JENNY.) Well, there's no need for you to loiter any longer. (*He finds himself automatically next the whiskey-bottle, and as automatically takes it up.*)

JENNY. Put that bottle down. And who gave you the right to give your orders?

EDWARD (*almost dropping the bottle*). I don't want any backchat from a bastard! . . .

JENNY. If you weren't an old man, and half drunk, I'd hit you for that!

FANNY. Stop being a fool, Edward. And leave that bottle alone, you sot!

EDWARD (*beginning to drivel*). You're all down on me, the whole lot of you. My God, we're in a mess. What the hell are we going to do?

FANNY. You must fend for yourself. I've looked after this house a long time now, and I daresay Adam'll want someone to look after it for him.

ARTHUR. Have we any money at all?

FANNY. What we've got in our pockets, I suppose.

JENNY (*to* ARTHUR). You'll be able to earn some now, with all that fancy education you've had.

[*The door opens and* DOREEN *enters, leading* KATE.

KATE (*protestingly*). For dear sake, Miss Doreen! . . .

DOREEN. Come on, now, Kate. Oh, where's Mr. Finlay?

JENNY. He's just gone.

FANNY. Sir Samuel left you five hundred pounds, Kate, and three pounds a week.

DOREEN. For life, Kate. And he thanks you for all you did for him, and says " God bless you, Kate! "

[KATE, *overcome, sits down in a chair, and cries.*

KATE. Oh, the kind man, the kind, kind man. Sure, I didn't do anything for him but what I was paid to do. I just did my work. But he was ever and always warm-natured, though his tongue was rough, an' him and me was the best of friends. I trust in God, the earth'll lie light on him, the kind, good man.

[ADAM *returns.*

FANNY. This house belongs now to Mr. Bothwell, Kate.

KATE (*so surprised that she forgets her tears*). Mr. Both-well? Not to you, then?

FANNY. No. Everything belongs to Mr. Bothwell. He's the master now.

DOREEN. You'll be able to retire and live in grandeur, Kate.

KATE. Me! Retire an' live in grandeur when I have my health an' strength about me. Dear O, child, I have my work to do. Who'd look after this place an' all of you if I was to take a notion of retirin' into my head?

ADAM. You'll stay here as long as you like, Kate.

KATE. Of course, I will. I'd like to see the person who would put me out. (*Looking at* JENNY.) Is this young lady stopping, too?

JENNY. No. I'm going now.

ADAM. This is Sir Sam's daughter, Kate.

KATE. Daughter!

ADAM. And she'll be treated as his daughter by every-body in this house.

KATE (*putting her hands on* JENNY'S *shoulders and*

peering at her). His daughter! Och, ay, you're the image of him. Why didn't he acknowledge you, daughter dear? It was comfort and company he needed, an' you'd 'a' given him both.

JENNY. Mebbe he had all the relations he wanted.

ADAM (*addressing them generally*). I don't see my way yet, but I'll think of something soon. All this fortune frightens me.

JENNY. I thought you liked money.

ADAM. I do. But this isn't money. It's finance.

FANNY. What about us, Adam. Arthur and Doreen and me—do you want us to go?

ADAM. Oh, no. Dear me, no.

FANNY (*as if making a decision for life*). Very well, then. We'll have a long talk presently . . . about everything.

ADAM. I'm most anxious to do what I can for you all! . . .

KATE (*glancing at the tray of refreshments*). Dear, oh dear, none of you has had any refreshments (*a glance at the whiskey bottle*) except Mr. Edward, of course. You never let Mr. Finlay go without offering him some refreshment. Oh, dear, oh dear! What hospitality! (*To Adam.*) Will I give you somethin', sir?

ADAM. No, thank you, Kate.

KATE. It's the custom, sir. Everybody takes a glass of wine at a funer'l. It's a nice custom . . . honourin' them that's gone.

ADAM. Oh, very well, then, Kate. I'll take some wine . . . a mouthful! . . .

KATE. There's port and sherry wine and whiskey—oh, dear, that's dwindled fearful—but port's the more customary, sir.

ADAM. I'll have port.

[KATE *pours a glass of wine for him. As she does so, she addresses the others.*]

KATE. Will I not pour out some wine for the rest of you?

ADAM. Yes, please do. A glass for each of us. And you'll have one yourself.

KATE (*delightedly pouring out the wine*). Well, yes, I

will, sir. I'm not a drinker, but when a person's buried, you must take a wee sup of wine.

ARTHUR. What for?

KATE. Oh, a tribute, Mr. Arthur, just a tribute. We can't let them go without a word or a sign. That wouldn't be like the thing at all. (*She carries the tray to* ADAM.) A glass of wine, sir.

ADAM (*taking one*). Thank you, Kate.

KATE. I hope you'll be long spared to live in this house.

ADAM. Thank you.

KATE (*turning to* MRS. CORKEN.) A glass of wine, mem. (MRS. CORKEN *takes a glass without speaking, and* KATE *passes on to* FANNY.) A glass of wine, mem.

FANNY. Thank you, Kate.

> [KATE *moves without speaking to* ARTHUR *and* DOREEN, *each of whom takes a glass.* EDWARD *comes forward and helps himself. Then* KATE *turns to* JENNY.]

KATE. A glass of wine, Miss Lepper.

JENNY. Lepper! Yes, I'll take a glass of wine, Kate, in my father's memory.

KATE. You're very like him in the face. It's as if I were standin' lookin' at him.

> [*She puts the tray on the table.*

ADAM. Where's your glass, Kate?

KATE. Oh, I . . . I haven't poured it out yet, sir.

ADAM (*going to where the decanters are*). Let me. (*He pours out a glass and hands it to her.*)

KATE. Thank you, Mr. Adam.

> [*She looks round, as if she expects them to say something, but no one does. They raise their glasses to their lips, following* ADAM'S *example, all except* KATE *who suddenly sits down, her glass untouched.*]

KATE. He was a kind man . . . an' an upright man . . . an' a very lonely man. (*She sips the wine.*) God bless his memory . . . the poor lonely old man.

> [*They finish their wine.*

ACT II

It is two months later, and we are again in the morning-room, which, however, looks brighter than when we last saw it, not so much because of changes in the furnishings as because of an evident desire for brightness in those who use it. The windows are open; the curtains are of livelier colour; and there are flowers in various parts of the room. The time is the afternoon. KATE *enters, accompanied by* JENNY CONN.

KATE. Oh, he's not here. I thought he was. Sit down, Miss Lepper.

JENNY. You mustn't call me that, Kate.

KATE. Och, how can I help it, an' you the dead spit of him. An' it should be your name by rights. I can't think where Mr. Adam can have got to. He was here a minute ago. Sit down an' I'll get him. He'll mebbe be up in his wee room, writin' or somethin'.

JENNY (*seating herself*). Is Mrs. Cairns in?

KATE. Och, indeed, she is. She's never out. There wasn't her equal for visitin' in Sir Sam's day, but these days she scarcely stirs out of the door.

JENNY. Is she sick or anything?

KATE. Och, dear, no! There isn't a happ'orth wrong with her. She just clings about the house, except when Mr. Adam goes out, an' then she seems always to have somethin' to do that takes her an' Miss Doreen along wi' him.

JENNY. Oh! Keeping an eye on him, eh?

KATE. I daresay you're right.

JENNY. Has Doreen a notion of him?

KATE. If she hasn't, her mother has. Before he knows where he is, that girl'll be married to him. Not, mind you, that there's anything behindhand wi' her. She's nice enough.

JENNY. Well, I suppose it's natural. They expected to get this house and most of the money, and if they didn't get it one way, you can't blame them for trying to get it another.

KATE (*dubiously*). No! Will I tell her you're here?

JENNY. Mrs. Cairns? No, thank you, Kate. Not yet, anyway. Mr. Bothwell wants to see me about some business or other. I'd better hear what he has to say without any interruption.

KATE. You'll be lucky if you do. Everything's overheard in this house these days. I feel like royalty sometimes, never able to budge wi'out someone at my elbow. (*As she glances out of the window.*) There's John James. I'll call him an' ask if he knows where the master is. (*At the window.*) John James! Come here a minute!

JOHN JAMES (*unseen*). What do you want?

KATE. Come here when I call you! (*To* JENNY.) He's an awful oul' man, this. He's been under notice this seven years, but he won't go. Has to have everything explained to him in words of one syllable afore he'll agree to it, an' then lets on he doesn't understan' a single word you're sayin'.

[JOHN JAMES GOURLAY *appears in the French window.* *He looks more ancient than he is, because of his brindled beard and thick, untidy hair, but his age is about the same as* KATE'S. *He's an obstinate, upright man, with a strong belief that there is an immense amount of wickedness in the world which it is his especial duty to expose.*]

JOHN JAMES. Were you wantin' me?

KATE. No, I'm just wearing me tongue out, callin' you. (*He turns to go.*) Here, come here!

JOHN JAMES (*turning back*). You said " No " when I asked were you wanting me.

KATE. I wish to my goodness, man, you'd learn sense an' not ask ignorant questions.

JOHN JAMES. Well, what are you wantin'?

KATE. Where's your manners, man? Don't you see Miss Lepper here?

JOHN JAMES. How're you, mem?

JENNY. I'm rightly, thank you, John James. I hope you are.

JOHN JAMES. Och, I'm not so bad. I've been worse.

KATE. You were never better, but things'll have to be superfect afore you'll acknowledge any good in them.

Dear pity the people on the Last Day. They'll get their ears warmed after you've had a look round.

JOHN JAMES. I thought you said you were wantin' me.

KATE. Ay, where's the master?

JOHN JAMES. How do I know? He's somewhere about.

KATE. Don't I know that. But where?

JOHN JAMES. Ah, down the garden or somewhere. I can't be responsible for people. Mebbe he's busy with this art he's so set on.

JENNY. Art?

JOHN JAMES. Ay! Plasterin' the place wi' art. There's a naked woman in the garden.

KATE. What in the earthly world are you talkin' about?

JOHN JAMES. On a ped-es-stall!

JENNY. Oh, a statue!

JOHN JAMES. Ay, but naked.

KATE. You had me heart in me mouth, you footerin' fool!

JOHN JAMES. Well, I'm tellin' you. I don't mind a bit of art in the Museum or the Free Lib'ry, or any place like that, but I object to it in a garden.

KATE. Away on now an' find him. Tell him Miss Lepper's here.

JENNY. Tell him Miss Conn's here.

JOHN JAMES. Make up your min' about it.

JENNY. Miss Conn.

JOHN JAMES. Right you are. Will I tell him anythin' else?

KATE. No. That'll be enough, unless you'd like to give in your notice over the head of the art.

JOHN JAMES (*scornfully*). Och! (*He turns away from the window, but a moment later turns back.*) Supposin' I don't see him?

KATE. Well, look for him 'til you do.

JOHN JAMES. But he might be some other place!

KATE. Och, go on, man, an' don't gab so much.

JOHN JAMES. Well, if I'm to go ploughin' all over the place, lookin' for people that should be here an' not there, I'll get behin' han' wi' me work. An' who'll be responsible for that?

KATE. You will.

JOHN JAMES. That's just what I thought! (*He goes away, grumbling.*)

JENNY. Is Mr. Bothwell making many changes, Kate?

KATE. Och, not many. The only way you can change a place like this is to tear it down. Besides, he's not let.

JENNY. Not let?

KATE. No, not a bit of it. The minute he tries to change anythin', a committee starts. You know, I suppose, that Mr. Edward an' Mrs. Corken are stoppin' here now?

JENNY. I didn't know *he* was.

KATE. Oh, ay, he's here all right. You don't catch that lad missin' anythin' that's goin'. He come 'til his tea yesterday was a fortnight, an' he's been here ever since.

JENNY. Then the whole of them are here?

KATE. Yes, the whole jim-bang of them . . . livin' on him.

JENNY. Well, they've always lived on somebody. I suppose it's his turn.

[DOREEN *enters.*

DOREEN. Oh, hillo, Jenny! I didn't know you were here. Have you come to stay?

JENNY (*laughing*). No, of course not.

DOREEN. Does mother know you're here?

JENNY. Not so far as I know. I've come to see Adam.

DOREEN. Oh, you'd better see mother.

JENNY. But I don't want to see her.

DOREEN. That doesn't matter. Mother likes to know all that's going on. Tell her, Kate.

KATE. I'm just goin' to hurry up the master, Miss Doreen. Mebbe, you'll stay here an' keep Miss Lepper in conversation. I'll not be a minute. (*And* KATE, *feeling very adroit, hurries out.*)

DOREEN. She *will* call you Miss Lepper. Mother tries hard to stop her, but it's useless.

JENNY. Yes. How are you, Doreen?

DOREEN. Oh, fit an' fizzin', as they say. Everythin's nicely settled now. Mother's got it all fixed. Of course, it's a nuisance having Aunt Essie and Uncle Edward, but she's over seventy, so she won't last long.

JENNY. Seventy's not old! She might easily last another ten or fifteen years.

DOREEN (*dismayed*). Oh, don't say that, Jenny! If I had my way, she wouldn't be here at all.

JENNY. *Your* way? Are you likely to get it?

DOREEN (*coyly*). I might. Mother thinks it would be the best for us all if Adam and I were . . . well! . . .

JENNY. You and Adam?

DOREEN. Uh-huh!

JENNY. There's a big difference between your ages. Does he know?

DOREEN. I dare say he suspects. Mother throws us together a lot. He likes me, you know.

JENNY. I'm sure he does. You're a likeable girl. Do you like him?

DOREEN. Yes, I do . . . a lot. I've always liked him. I don't think it matters much that he's older than I am. Girls have to marry men older than themselves now. Boys their own age can't afford to marry them. Mind you, Jenny, if I do marry Adam, I'll soon clear this lot out.

JENNY. The whole lot?

DOREEN. Yes . . . mother included. I think I'd better tell her you're here. She'll be jumping mad if she isn't told.

JENNY. She won't jump any madder if you wait a while. Where's Arthur?

DOREEN. Putting somebody right, I suppose. I'm very fond of Arthur, but I wish he wasn't always telling me about everything.

JENNY. But, Doreen, dear, he's just heard about them, and, of course, he's anxious to tell us all. He thinks we don't know. What'll you do if Adam doesn't marry you?

DOREEN. I can't think. We're dependent on him.

JENNY. Get a job, Doreen.

DOREEN. I'd rather get married.

[KATE *enters.*

KATE. Here's the master now.

DOREEN. I'd better leave you, then.

JENNY. Yes, and don't tell your mother I'm here. Not yet anyway. Go for a walk.

DOREEN. I've had two walks this morning already.

JENNY. Well, have another. Third time lucky.

[ADAM *enters.*

ADAM. How're you Jenny?

DOREEN. Well, good-bye for the present. (*She strokes* ADAM'S *arm as she passes him on the way out.*)

KATE (*to* JENNY). You'll stay to your tea, I suppose?

ADAM. Yes. Yes, of course, she will.

[KATE *goes out and* ADAM *pulls a chair close to* JENNY'S *and sits down.*]

ADAM. I hope you're well, Jenny.

JENNY. I'm the best, Adam.

ADAM. I wish you'd come oftener to see us. You know you're welcome.

JENNY. Yes, I know. What a nice girl Doreen is.

ADAM (*disinterestedly*). Doreen! Oh, yes. Yes, she's quite a nice girl!

JENNY. Young and very attractive.

ADAM. A bit too young, don't you think?

JENNY. Oh, Adam, nobody can be too young!

ADAM. Can't they? Some people are never anything else.

JENNY. But you must like Doreen. She's nice-looking and good-natured.

ADAM. That's all she is.

JENNY. Well, that's a lot, isn't it?

ADAM. Perhaps. But I like people to be adult. However, I like her well enough. Much better than Arthur.

JENNY. That's not saying much.

ADAM. Well, better than any of the others.

JENNY. That's not saying much either. I hear you've got the house full?

ADAM (*with a wry smile*). Yes, we are rather numerous!

JENNY (*teasing him*). I'd better come and complete the number.

ADAM (*sincerely*). I wish you would. Why don't you?

JENNY (*genially*). Oh, Adam, don't be daft. With Aunt Essie and Edward and Fanny and the rest and me, this house would be hell. What do you want to see me about?

ADAM. Ah, that's important. It's about the money, Jenny. I'm making up my mind to divide it equally between us.

D

JENNY. Us?

ADAM. Yes . . . all of us. You're to have the same share as the rest.

JENNY (*after a pause—deeply touched*). That's very nice of you, Adam.

ADAM. I don't think so. If justice were done, you'd have the lot. You see, Jenny, I feel very awkward about all this wealth. It doesn't suit me to be as rich as this. I'm easily contented. I only want . . . enough.

JENNY. So does everybody. But what is enough?

ADAM. In my case, very little. There's another thing. I don't feel that I have any right to the money. Sir Samuel must have been in a very strange state when he made that will. I don't like to take advantage of the dead.

JENNY. He wasn't out of his mind, Adam.

ADAM. No, I don't think he was. But he was feeling sour. I can't believe he really meant to do nothing at all for the rest of his family, and I'm sure, wherever he is now, he'll feel happier if I put things right. There's a lot more in this family business than you and I think, Jenny. It's a good model for life. We're not all equal, but we *belong*. Tommy isn't stinted because he's not as clever as Willie. They both *belong*. I mean, Jenny, we don't give Tommy less to eat than his brother Willie because Willie won a scholarship and Tommy didn't. See what I mean? I don't think people should be penalized because they aren't as brilliant as other people. After all, being brilliant's an accident. We don't make ourselves clever or stupid.

JENNY. Some of us do. Edward, for example.

ADAM. Yes, but broadly speaking, Jenny. And, of course, Tommy may turn out in the end to be much more brilliant than Willie. It's a matter of development, isn't it? Anyhow, a good father will treat all his children alike and chance what happens.

JENNY. That's not my view.

ADAM. Oh, Jenny, you wouldn't discriminate between one child and another.

JENNY. Yes, I would. If I had a clever son and a son that was a fool, I'd give the clever one advantages I wouldn't dream of giving the fool. That would be worse than silly : it would be wasteful. Have you told the others yet?

ADAM. No.

JENNY. Don't. You mustn't divide the fortune. If father'd wanted that, he'd have divided it himself. You can do something with a fortune if it's kept together, but you can't do anything if you split it. I'm all against division, Adam. Splitting and splitting until there's nothing left to split. Father wanted his money kept together and used. What'll Edward do with his share? Drink himself stupider than he is. I can't tell you how I despise that man. God gave him some sort of a brain, but what's he done with it? Soaked it in drink. If he were to drop dead at my feet this minute, I wouldn't turn a hair.

ADAM. You make yourself sound very hard.

JENNY. I *am* hard, Adam. We need hard people here. You know, there's a great difference between you and me. You've never been really poor. I have.

ADAM. But Sir Sam provided for your mother.

JENNY. Oh, Adam, nobody on earth could have provided for my mother. Money melted in her hand. It isn't always poverty that's the matter with people: it's themselves. Father provided for her all right, but she didn't provide for herself. We had the bailiffs in more than once, but he got them out. I think she bored him, Adam. She bored me, and I'm very like him.

ADAM. Yes, you are. How strange it is that he never realized how much you were his daughter.

JENNY. But he did. We were too much alike to get on together. He tried to be friends with me, tried hard, but I wouldn't let him. I told him once he'd got me into trouble as much as my mother, and I'd see myself out of it. He didn't like that.

ADAM. Too proud, Jenny, too proud.

JENNY. I'm an Ulsterwoman, Adam. The upshot of it all was, we had more downs than ups. The ups were all right as long as they lasted, but they didn't last long enough. It's a terrible thing to despise your mother. I despised mine. I was fond of her, but I'd no respect for her. She slithered through her life. There was one time when things were desperate for us. That was when I told my father what I thought of him, and wouldn't let her go next or near him. I preferred to go hungry! . . .

ADAM. As bad as that?

JENNY. Yes, as bad as that! It wasn't funny to be hungry, Adam. Father was raging mad when he found out. I will say that for him, he was desperately anxious about us, and especially about me. It was then he made the arrangement about money with Mr. Finlay that lasted 'til my mother died.

ADAM. He didn't stop it, did he?

JENNY. No, I did. I've kept myself ever since. Do you remember saying one day you had no illusions about the rich?

ADAM. Uh-huh!

JENNY. I can go one better than that, Adam. I have no illusions about the poor. You see, I've been one.

ADAM. But I've never been one of the rich . . . until now.

JENNY. You've never been one of the rich or poor. That's why you have illusions about them. So has that silly fool, Arthur. He strikes me as the perfect example of an intellectual gumph. He knows too much! . . .

ADAM. He'll know less as he grows older.

JENNY. I hope so. The queer thing is, that although I fought with my father, and went against him every way I could, I loved him. I'd 'a' given the world to 'a' been his acknowledged daughter. I did love him! (*She is overcome by emotion, and for a moment cannot continue. But she recovers and goes on.*) I used to stand and look at him sometimes, when he didn't know I was there, and I'd feel my heart lifting when I saw what a masterful man he was. Money didn't make him, Adam: he made money. He'd have been just as masterful if he hadn't had tuppence in his pocket.

ADAM. He had his weakness, too, Jenny. That letter he left was a weak letter.

JENNY. I daresay. But it was the weakness of a man that's strong, not the weakness of a man that's weak. That's why I don't want you to divide his fortune. Keep it together, Adam. I hate disunity and division.

ADAM. He did me a great injury when he left me his money. I was a happy man until I got it. I bothered nobody, and nobody bothered me. I did my day's work, pleasing myself if I pleased no other person, and I was satisfied.

JENNY. Too satisfied.

ADAM. But I wronged no one. I deprived nobody. I kept in my own corner and earned my living in my own way. And I was happy. But now I'm a burdened man. I have to be responsible for people who will not be responsible for themselves. I don't want to be my brother's keeper, but I am compelled to be. Every post brings me batches of letters from spongers. Do this for me, do that for me, give me this, that and the other. I feel sorry for Sir Sam when I think he had years of it, but I feel sorrier for myself when I think that I may have even more years of it than he had.

JENNY. But don't you like making people do what you want them to do?

ADAM. No. There's a man in my garden who fought in France in the last war. He refused, time after time, to take stripes and promotion because they'd separate him from his comrades, and he liked his comrades better than he liked promotion. I feel like that. Every rise a man gets takes him away from the people he likes. He has to remember his position and his dignity. They mustn't be familiar with him, lest they take a liberty. If he visits them, he feels he's conferring a favour on them, and they feel that, too. Then the visits cease. In place of the old friendly relation, there comes a coolness, a distant nod instead of a kindly greeting, a realization on each side of his importance and their insignificance, and at last, a break that is almost enmity. What's worse still, Jenny, is having to profess friendship for people you can't bear.

JENNY. Oh, but getting the better of them, Adam!

ADAM. I don't want to get the better of them. I want them to get the better of me. What's getting the better of a man but tricking him, humbugging him, deceiving him, cheating him. But if I let him get the better of me, he gets the best I have.

JENNY. You're an odd fellow.

ADAM. Do you mean I'm a foolish one?

JENNY. No. No, I don't think that, Adam. You're not a fool, but you're odd. If everybody thought as you think, there'd be no unity! . . .

ADAM. Is unity a good thing?

JENNY. You can't doubt that, Adam?

ADAM. But I do. I don't object to the unity of different people for the same purpose, if each of them wants that purpose, but I do object to it if it means that I have to like what you like, whether I want it or not.

JENNY. You ought to live on a desert island.

ADAM. Sometimes I think that myself, but unfortunately, Jenny, I like people. That's why I've no wish to be rich and powerful. I'm afraid I shall have to stop liking people and start making them do things. And then they'll hate me. I shall have great possessions, but no friends.

JENNY. That's the way of the world. There have to be cattle, and there have to be drivers! . . .

ADAM. Then the world must go its own way and leave me to go mine. I'm not very well acquainted with cattle-drivers, but the little I do know of them makes me like cattle. Have you ever looked at a cattle-driver, Jenny, looked close at him?

JENNY. I know what you mean. They're not nice men.

ADAM. No, they're not nice men. Yet you want me to become one. No, thank you, Jenny. Every man in this world is unique. There never was anybody like him before, and there'll never be anybody like him again. He has his own gift for the world, and nobody but he can give it.

JENNY. You're here to fit into the plan; you're not here to throw it out of order.

ADAM. I don't like that theory. I'm not a cog in a wheel. I'm a thought in the mind of God.

JENNY. What's the difference? No, no, Adam, all that's just talk. You're trying to run away from your responsibilities, and you're making fine excuses for yourself, but they're only excuses, and you are running away. That's not manly. I saw a play once, a terrible piece about a boy who wouldn't grow up. He dodged his duty.

ADAM. And what was his duty?

JENNY. To grow up and be a man and do a man's job and bear a man's burden; to live like a man, and not like a child.

[*Enter* ARTHUR.

ARTHUR. Oh! Am I intruding?

JENNY. Yes.

ARTHUR (*disconcerted almost for the first time in his life*). Oh, sorry! I thought, perhaps, tea was ready! . . .

JENNY. It isn't.

ARTHUR. Oh, well, then! . . . (*He retires in embarrassment, uttering nervous sniggers as if he were trying to make the best of a very bad business*).

ADAM (*laughing with delight*). Sir Sam couldn't have improved on that. You're his daughter all right.

JENNY. Adam, listen to me—you can do more with the money if you keep it intact. Don't divide it.

[FANNY *enters.*

FANNY. How are you, Miss Conn. I didn't know until now that you were here. Arthur told me.

JENNY. Arthur's a very communicative young man. I hope I didn't disturb you.

FANNY. Oh, you wouldn't have been disturbing me. You'll stay to tea, of course. Shall I ring, Adam? You've finished your . . . conversation, I suppose?

ADAM. Yes, I think we might have tea.

FANNY (*as she rings*). Been busy?

ADAM. No, not very. I've been in the garden most of the morning.

FANNY (*briskly bright*). I expect you had a lot to say to Miss Conn?

JENNY. Yes, we had a good deal to say, Fanny, and we said it.

FANNY (*slightly dashed*). Hmmm! (*Then she rallies.*) Adam and I discuss everything together. Don't we, Adam?

ADAM. Do we?

FANNY. Yes, of course, we do. I tell you all my troubles, and I like you to tell me yours. We must help each other. If relations can't confide in each other, what can they do?

JENNY. They can mind their own business.

FANNY. But, surely, that is their business. (KATE *enters.*) Oh, we'll have tea, Kate.

KATE. Very good, mem. Will I tell Mrs. Corken and Mr. Scantlebury?

FANNY. Yes, when it's ready. Not before. (KATE *goes*

out, and FANNY, *after looking over her shoulder to see that the door is closed, continues.*) Adam, you really must get rid of Kate. She's much too old for this work, and she's far too familiar. She was rude just now to Arthur.

ADAM. I'm sometimes tempted to be rude to Arthur myself. Kate has good manners. He must have provoked her.

FANNY. Nonsense. How can our class be rude to her class? Arthur is just a high-spirited boy, a little over-educated, perhaps, but that'll wear off. It won't be any hardship to get rid of Kate. She's well provided for—better than I am—and she *is too old*. We ought to have a smart-looking parlour-maid. Really, in your position, Adam, you ought to have a butler ! . . .

ADAM. A what?

FANNY. A butler. We don't use nearly enough men-servants in this country. Why, I don't know. It isn't as if there weren't plenty of unemployed. The French are a democratic people, if that's a virtue, but they use men-servants everywhere. I'm all for it. Men cook much better than women ! . . .

ADAM. You're not going to suggest a chef, are you?

FANNY. No, but why not? People ought to live up to their position. I don't like this modern notion of a king who behaves like a corner-boy. You agree with me, Miss Conn? Adam ought to live up to his position?

JENNY. Don't ask me, Fanny. I don't know what his position is.

FANNY. You know how much money he has. A rich man ought to spend as much of his income as he can. It's our duty to live as well as possible. That's civilization . . . living well and making a good display. I used to say that to Uncle Sam, but he wouldn't listen to me. What's the use of being a millionaire when you live like a civil servant? You really ought to get a butler, Adam. Any-how, Kate ought to go.

ADAM. I'll tell her what you say ! . . .

FANNY (*dismayed*). Oh, please, don't. I don't want her to think that I'm trying to get rid of her.

JENNY. But you *are*.

FANNY. Isn't this a private matter, Miss Conn?

ADAM. Jenny's a member of this family, Fanny.

FANNY. Oh, yes, of course . . . in a way. I'm thinking of Kate's interests as much as Henry's. *She is too old* for this work. Do you know what her age is?

ADAM. I don't think of age when I think of Kate.

FANNY. You ought to. She's sixty. It's not right to have a woman of that age working.

JENNY. There are millions of them doing it.

FANNY. Common humanity, apart from common-sense, makes me feel that Kate ought to be resting. You'd better think it over, Adam.

ADAM. I have.

FANNY. I know an excellent butler, a most worthy man, who will shortly be disengaged. I was going to suggest he should come over to-morrow to see you.

ADAM. But I don't want to waste his time.

FANNY. You won't be wasting it. Those sort of people haven't so much to do that their time can be wasted. (KATE *enters, pushing a tea-waggon.*) Have you told the others, Kate?

KATE. Yes, mem. (*She puts the waggon in front of* FANNY.) I didn't see Mr. Scantlebury.

FANNY. I don't suppose he'll want any tea. That's another thing I want to talk to you about, Adam.

KATE. There's plenty for him if he does come in.

JENNY. He says tea's the curse of Ireland.

KATE. It doesn't trouble him much. (*To* FANNY.) Have you got everything?

FANNY. I'll ring if I haven't.

> [DOREEN *and* ARTHUR *enter.* KATE *goes out.* FANNY *busies herself distributing the tea which* ARTHUR *and* DOREEN *take to the others.*]

ADAM. Well, Arthur, what have you been doing for suffering humanity to-day?

ARTHUR. You know, Adam, you're like a lot of people—flippant.

FANNY (*very sharply*). Arthur! Arthur! Remember to whom you're talking.

ADAM. That's all right, Fanny. I like being put in my place by my juniors. Go on, Arthur, tell me my faults.

DOREEN. He never tells anybody anything else.

ARTHUR. I'm serious, but scarcely anybody else is. I doubt if there's ever been a more flippant age than this. Everybody makes jokes. Ha, ha, ha! when they should be crying. Everything's such fun. Laugh, clown, laugh. And because I try to think seriously about things, I'm derided and jeered at.

FANNY. As I've told you more than once, Arthur, you're a prig.

DOREEN. And a bore.

ARTHUR. There! That's all the answer you get when you try to be serious. You're called a prig and a bore and asked to fiddle while Rome burns.

ADAM (*to* JENNY). You mustn't jest while Arthur's about. If you do, he'll write to *The New Statesman* about it.

JENNY. Never mind, Arthur. I'm a prig, too. Come and sit beside me. (*He does so.*) What are you going to do?

ARTHUR. I haven't quite made up my mind yet. I'm going into politics, of course, but whether in Ireland or England, I haven't decided.

ADAM. Why don't you lead Southern Ireland back to the North? That would be a great benefit to suffering humanity.

ARTHUR. I'd like to put romantic Ireland with O'Leary in the grave, and when it's there, I hope it'll stay there.

ADAM. Won't you leave us a little light and colour, Arthur? (MRS. CORKEN *enters.*) Oh, hillo, Aunt. (*He rises to put a chair for her.*)

MRS. CORKEN. Thank you, Adam. (*To* JENNY.) Is that you?

JENNY. How are you, Aunt Essie?

MRS. CORKEN. Och, I'm just middling. Better than some people like, though. What were you all talking about when I came in?

ADAM. Arthur doesn't think we're serious enough.

MRS. CORKEN. 'Deed, he's right! Brothers willing their money away from their own relations. Where's Edward?

DOREEN. Out somewhere.

MRS. CORKEN. I told him to get me something in town

I wanted, but I forget now what it was, and I'm dead sure
he's forgot, too, so now I'll never get it. Nobody cares
whether I live or die.

FANNY (*as she hands her a cup of tea*). Now, now, now,
Aunt Essie. You mustn't talk like that. That's naughty.

MRS. CORKEN. Well, I am old, you know. You can't
get away from that. Seventy-one I'll be the twenty-eighth
of September next. Ay! Seventy-one. (*Takes a sip of
the tea.*) Did you put any sugar in this?

FANNY. Yes. Two lumps.

MRS. CORKEN. That's not sugar. I like four lumps.
(FANNY *gives her the extra lumps.*) I know I'm a trouble
and a botheration . . . you having to maintain me, Adam,
when my own brother didn't provide for me . . . but I
won't trouble you much longer.

ADAM (*endeavouring to cheer her up*). Oh, indeed, you
will!

MRS. CORKEN. No, no, my time's nearly up. Ay, ay!
Every night I get down on my bended knees and beg God
not to let me be a botheration. Give me one of those wee
cakes, Fanny! Oh, God, I say, don't let me be a botheration to anybody. (FANNY *passes the plate of cakes to her,
and she takes one and bites into it.*) Och, I don't like this
cake. Haven't you one with sugar on it?

FANNY. I'm sorry, Aunt Essie. Kate didn't bring any
in.

MRS. CORKEN. Well, ring, will you, and ask her if she
has any of those fancy cakes with sugar on them. You do
it, Doreen, dear. (DOREEN *does it.*) Kate's getting very
neglectful lately. She knows rightly I like a sugary cake
for my tea. It's not much I want, but I think I might be
let have a wee bun with sugar on it. But there I'm old in
years. You can't get away from that. Oh, God, I pray
every night, don't let me be a botheration to nobody.

DOREEN. Do you believe prayer's ever answered, aunt?

MRS. CORKEN. Well, sometimes it is, and sometimes it
isn't. I often think God's not as discriminating as He
might be. (EDWARD *enters.*) You're late for your tea,
Edward!

EDWARD. Och, it doesn't bother me to be late for that.
What have you?

FANNY. Tea. What does one usually have for tea?

EDWARD. Not funny! Not funny at all. (*Takes a piece of bread and begins to munch it.*) How are you, Jenny?

JENNY. Bravely, thank you. How are you?

EDWARD. Not so bad, not so bad!

MRS. CORKEN. Isn't that woman ever coming? Ring again, somebody.

[ARTHUR *rings the bell for* KATE.

EDWARD (*to* JENNY). What brings you here?

JENNY. Our host.

EDWARD. Host! Oh, yes, yes! Adam, of course. Heth, it sounds funny to hear him called that. D'you hear what she called you, Adam? The host.

ADAM. Well, in a way, I might be called that, mightn't I? You've done me the honour to extend your visit! . . .

EDWARD (*sobered*). I hope I haven't outstayed my welcome.

[KATE *enters.*

KATE. Yes, mem?

MRS. CORKEN. Kate, are there none of those wee fancy cakes with sugar on the top of them?

KATE. Mary didn't bake any!

MRS. CORKEN (*almost devastated*). Och, dear, oh dear, oh dear. And why not? Doesn't she know rightly I like them?

KATE. I don't know. She just didn't bake any.

FANNY. All right, Kate. [*Exit* KATE.

MRS. CORKEN. It's a queer thing when a woman my age can't get a wee fancy cake for her tea. God knows, it's not much I want, but even that I can't get. Ah, well! Have you any other kind of a cake, Fanny, besides the one I didn't like. . . .

[*She begins to pry among the cakes, and we can leave her to it for a while.*]

ADAM. Now that we're all here, I want to say to you what I've just been saying to Jenny. Ever since I inherited Sir Sam's fortune, I've been turning over in my mind what I'll do with it.

FANNY (*puzzled, but suspicious*). Oh yes, Adam!

ADAM. Jenny, I may tell you, doesn't approve of my plan.

MRS. CORKEN. What's it got to do with her, anyway?

ADAM (*disregarding her*). I haven't made up my mind definitely yet. Jenny's disturbed my thoughts. But I want to consult you.

EDWARD. Anything I can do, of course! . . .

ARTHUR. As a matter of fact, Adam, I've drafted a scheme for the disposal of a fortune . . . I don't mean yours in particular, but any fortune . . . and I'll let you have a look at it, if you like.

ADAM. Thank you, Arthur. That's very kind of you.

ARTHUR. Not at all. It's just part of my general scheme for settling things.

DOREEN. I don't see why you shouldn't keep the money and spend it the way you want to. It's yours, isn't it?

ARTHUR (*despairingly*). I've spent hours instructing that girl in the principles of political economy, and she's still talking like that. I've lent her books by G. D. H. Cole.

DOREEN. I couldn't read them.

ADAM. I rather like his detective stories, Doreen.

ARTHUR. Obsolete individualism, that's her creed, as far as she has one. Sometimes, I despair of women! . . .

FANNY. What's your scheme, Adam?

ADAM. I thought of dividing the money among us equally.

EDWARD. That's an idea!

FANNY. Equally?

ADAM. Yes.

MRS. CORKEN. I'd like to know a wee bit more about this. Who do you mean by " us "?

ADAM. All who are in this room.

MRS. CORKEN. Does that include Miss Conn?

ADAM. Yes. Strictly speaking she ought to have the lot . . . more, anyhow, than the rest of us.

MRS. CORKEN. I don't see that at all. You're putting the wages of sin very high, Adam. And are these two children here (*she indicates* ARTHUR *and* DOREEN) to get the same share as me and Edward and you?

ADAM. Ye-es, that was in my mind!

MRS. CORKEN. That wouldn't be fair at all. I don't call that just or right.

EDWARD. Come to think of it, there's something in

what Aunt Essie says. If the money's divided equally, me and you and Jenny here and Aunt Essie'll only get a seventh, but Fanny and her children'll get nearly half of it.

MRS. CORKEN. The children ought to be left out altogether . . . except, mebbe, for a present of a hundred or two. They can get Fanny's share between them when she dies. The right way to deal with the fortune is to split it between Edward and Fanny and me and you, Adam. There's no call for anybody else to have a share.

EDWARD. I wouldn't be against you keeping a bit extra for yourself, as a bonus, you might say, for your sacrifice.

MRS. CORKEN. What sacrifice will it be? He'll be doing what's right in the eyes of God, and he'll have plenty left for himself, far more nor he ever anticipated.

ADAM. I never anticipated any.

MRS. CORKEN. Well, there you are.

ADAM. What do you think, Fanny?

FANNY. I don't know yet, Adam. It wants thinking about.

ARTHUR. If you ask me ! . . .

ADAM. But I'm not asking you, Arthur. (*Collapse of* ARTHUR.) Don't you think I'm doing right to divide the fortune, Fanny?

FANNY. I'm not sure. Of course, we'll do well if you divide it as you propose, but I'm not sure that I . . . I must think it over.

ADAM. Are you like Jenny? She thinks I oughtn't to divide it.

FANNY. Why?

JENNY. Because my father left it to him, and not to us. He didn't want it divided away to nothing. He wanted it kept together. If Adam splits the fortune, what'll it amount to among us?

MRS. CORKEN. Enough for me, anyway.

EDWARD. It'll get me through nicely.

JENNY. Yes. Get you through. That's all it'll do. But that's not enough. (*Turning to Adam.*) Do you think my father toiled and moiled for that money only to have it squandered by a doting old woman and a drunkard.

[*There's an uproar at once.*

MRS. CORKEN. What do you mean, you terge? . . .

ADAM (*above the din*). Aunt Essie! Aunt Essie!

MRS. CORKEN. It's a nice thing when an old woman of seventy has to sit still and hear herself called out of her name by a . . . bastard.

JENNY (*restraining* ADAM, *who is about to speak angrily*). All right, Adam, I deserved that.

EDWARD. Is there any need to keep on referring to me as if I were a chronic drunkard? I admit I take a drink or two. Who wouldn't, these times? But I object to being talked about as if I ought to be in a home for alcoholics.

JENNY. I'm sorry I spoke the way I did, but that's how I feel. If this money is to do any good, it ought to be kept in one sum and not divided and made useless. What'll Aunt Essie do with her share? Or you?

MRS. CORKEN. I know rightly what I'll do with mine. Spend it the way it ought to be spent. Providing for my declining years.

JENNY. Is that all? Easing an old woman into the grave?

EDWARD. I'm not under any obligation to say what I'll do with my share. If I choose to waste it, that's my business, and no other body's.

JENNY. But you didn't earn it, and you've no right to waste what you didn't make.

ARTHUR. I still think that if you were to look at my draft scheme for the disposal of private fortunes! . . .

ADAM. Keep it until you have one to dispose of.

DOREEN. How would it do, Adam, if you were to make us each an allowance? Then you wouldn't need to divide the money. Do people pay income tax on allowances?

ADAM. I don't know. I'd have to pay, of course, but I don't suppose the Government would make you pay.

EDWARD. Wouldn't they, begod? The Government's the biggest robber on earth. If the like of us was to do a tenth of the things the Government does, we'd be hanged, drawn and quartered. And instead of trying to curb their power, this fellow (*indicating* ARTHUR) wants to increase it. They take the bite out of your mouth, and then gaol you for tasting it.

DOREEN (*to* ADAM). Well, how would it be if you were

to divide the income between us, after you've paid the tax? Then you could satisfy both yourself *and* Jenny.

MRS. CORKEN. That wouldn't be any better than the first idea. You three would be better off than the rest of us. And supposing Adam was to take it into his head to stop the allowance? Or was to die without a will? Where would we be, then? (*To* ADAM.) Who's your next of kin?

ADAM. I think you are.

MRS. CORKEN. Oh, then, in that case! . . .

JENNY. You can leave me out of this. I'm against division, and I won't take a penny piece of your money.

ADAM. Oh, but Jenny, you're his child! . . .

JENNY. That's why. I've only to look into my own mind to know what was in his. He wanted something done with his money : he didn't want it wasted.

EDWARD. Are you suggesting we'd waste it?

JENNY. Yes. You especially. These ones won't do anything with it, Adam. Divide it now, and where'll it be in two or three years? Aunt Essie'll be dead! . . .

MRS. CORKEN. Not if I can help it. I'm in no hurry to meet my God.

FANNY. There's no need to decide anything now. You've mentioned your idea, Adam, and now let us think it over. I'm inclined to agree with Miss Conn that the money should not be divided.

ARTHUR. You might start a weekly review with me as editor. Ireland badly needs an intelligent paper. There are any amount of brains lying about unassembled in this country. I can assemble them if I'm financed and given a free hand.

JENNY. Is there anything else you want to say to me, Adam?

ADAM. No, thank you, Jenny. Except that I wish you'd come here oftener. I need your advice. There's this house, for instance. What am I to do with it?

JENNY. Pull it down.

MRS. CORKEN. Girl! Girl! Have you no respect or reverence. This is an old house . . . older'n my father and mother.

JENNY. I don't like old houses. Pull them down and build new ones. Good-bye, Adam.

ADAM. I'll come to the door with you!

ARTHUR. I wish you'd think over my suggestion of a weekly review. You couldn't do better than start an independent organ of opinion! . . .

[*But* JENNY *and* ADAM *have left the room without paying any heed to* ARTHUR.]

EDWARD. That's a terrible woman!

FANNY. Who? Miss Conn?

EDWARD. Oh, stop calling her Miss Conn. Why can't you call her by her name, the same as the rest of us?

FANNY. I'll choose my own friends, Edward. I won't let you choose them for me.

MRS. CORKEN. You're right, Edward! She's a terrible girl! No respect or reverence! None!

ARTHUR. She's an iconoclast.

EDWARD. What the hell's that?

MRS. CORKEN. Can't you talk English, Arthur?

DOREEN. He's learning Gaelic.

ARTHUR. A destroyer of idols. I admire her for that. I'm one myself.

MRS. CORKEN. Are you calling us idols?

ARTHUR. Figuratively speaking, yes. I'm interested in that woman. There's something in her. She has a lower middle-class outlook on life, of course, and that's out of place in Ireland. There are only two points of view in this country—aristocratic and peasant. The rest don't count.

MRS. CORKEN. You're a terrible blatherskite, boy.

EDWARD. You'd look well if you were married to her.

ARTHUR. Marriage doesn't come within my purview!

MRS. CORKEN. Didn't I tell you to speak English. (*To* EDWARD.) That woman's more likely to marry Adam than Arthur.

FANNY. Adam! Did you say Adam?

MRS. CORKEN. Of course I said Adam. You don't suppose I said Edward. Have you no eyes in your head?

FANNY. But he's very fond of Doreen!

MRS. CORKEN. Not at all. *Not at all!*

FANNY. You think he's fond of you, Doreen?

DOREEN. I think he likes me. And I like him.

MRS. CORKEN. I like John the Baptist, but I wouldn't 'a' married him.

E

FANNY. Has Adam said anything to make you think he wants to marry her?

MRS. CORKEN. He doesn't need to say anything. I have eyes in my head. That sort of man is meat and drink to that sort of woman. Besides, Fanny, Doreen's far too young for him.

FANNY. She's not in the least too young. Men of his age are often devoted to girls of hers.

MRS. CORKEN. Not Adam. Edward, mebbe, but not Adam. You mark my words, the whole of you, whoever marries Adam, it won't be Doreen. I'll take my Bible oath on that. It'll likely be her. (*She jerks her thumb in the direction* JENNY *has just taken.*) Well, well, I can do no more good down here! (*She gets up from her chair.*)

EDWARD. You haven't done any.

MRS. CORKEN. Would you recognize good if you saw it?

EDWARD. Any backs there were to raise in this room, you raised. And you have Fanny near in hysterics with all this talk of Adam marrying Jenny.

FANNY. I'm not in the least hysterical, Edward. The whole idea is too fantastic.

MRS. CORKEN (*tottering towards the door*). Well, I'm telling you. That's all. Look out for yourselves! . . .

[*She goes out muttering to herself that she's telling them.*]

EDWARD. Sometimes, when I listen to Aunt Essie, I wonder why God made the human race. You know everything, Arthur. Tell me that?

ARTHUR. I dislike people who are always trying to be funny!

[*And out of the French window he goes.* DOREEN *follows him as far as the window, where she stands watching him walking off into the garden.*]

EDWARD. Bumptious ass! How in the name of God, Fanny, did you come to produce that fellow?

FANNY. In the customary way, Edward. Can't you think of anything better to do than insult my son?

EDWARD (*getting up*). What direction is he going, Doreen?

DOREEN. Up towards the planting.

EDWARD. Thank you! I'll go the opposite way. (*To*

FANNY.) If Adam says any more to you about splitting the fortune, encourage him. I'm all for it.

FANNY. I'm not. I agree with that woman, Conn. It ought to be kept together.

EDWARD. Kept together! For who? Her or us?

[*She doesn't reply, and he goes out by the door.*

FANNY. Doreen!

DOREEN. Yes, mother.

FANNY. Come here a minute!

DOREEN (*as she comes into the room*). What do you want, mother?

FANNY. Has Adam made love to you?

DOREEN. Not what I'd call love. But then I'm younger than he is.

FANNY. Do you think he wants to marry you?

DOREEN. How do I know? I hope he does. I'd like to be married.

FANNY. Do you love him?

DOREEN. Och, mother, don't ask so many questions.

FANNY. Don't be foolish, child. I'm not asking for fun. It's important, this. Do you love him?

DOREEN. Well, I wouldn't mind being married to him, if that's what you mean, so I suppose I must love him. But I don't feel what I'd call a grand passion for him.

FANNY. Would it hurt you if he were to marry another woman?

DOREEN. I'd feel annoyed.

FANNY. You obviously don't love him. I've got to think what to do, and it depends on how you feel about him. You see, Doreen, we must control that money somehow. I want it kept together for us. I don't care how you get it as long as you do. Can't you . . . make him marry you!

DOREEN. Mother, what on earth are you saying?

FANNY. Can't you make him marry you—that's what I'm saying.

DOREEN. How can I?

FANNY. How does any girl make a man marry her? There are ways, aren't there?

DOREEN. I don't know how. And if I did, I wouldn't. I'm not going to force anybody to marry me. If he doesn't want me, I don't want him.

FANNY. I've a good mind to ask him outright.

DOREEN. For dear sake, mother, don't. I'll die of shame if you do.

FANNY. You'd better go now. He may come back any minute, and I want to talk to him.

DOREEN. About me?

FANNY. About everything.

DOREEN (*hesitating*). Well! . . .

FANNY. Go 'long, dear!

DOREEN (*tearfully*). You're terrible, mother, terrible!

[*She rushes out of the room into the house.* FANNY *stands still for a moment or two, looking after her, and then, as if she had heard a sound, walks towards the French window and looks out. She sees* ADAM, *and calls.*]

FANNY. Adam! Ad-am! (*He is heard replying.*) Come this way.

[*She returns to the centre of the room, and a moment or two later,* ADAM *enters.*]

ADAM. Yes, Fanny?

FANNY. Seen her off?

ADAM. Who? Jenny? Oh, yes. Several minutes ago.

FANNY. Adam, I want to speak to you!

ADAM. Uh-huh!

FANNY. It's about something very important.

ADAM. Yes?

FANNY (*seating herself*). Sit down a minute. I can't talk to you when you're standing. (*He seats himself.*) Aunt Essie thinks you're going to be married! . . .

ADAM. Married? Me?

FANNY. Yes. She thinks your talk just now shows that you want to settle down.

ADAM. More like settling up, don't you think?

FANNY (*laughing bleakly*). That's what I thought. But Aunt Essie is convinced you're going to marry Miss Conn.

ADAM. What put that idea into her head?

FANNY. I can't tell you. Edward said your heart was set on Doreen.

ADAM. Doreen! Our little Doreen! My dear Fanny, I hope you stamped on him for that.

FANNY. He was teasing her, of course. I was very vexed

about it. Edward has a queer sense of humour. It's usually misplaced. I didn't think it funny myself.

ADAM. Oh, but I think it's extremely funny. Doreen must have been amused. What a comic idea! I must chaff her about it.

FANNY. No, don't do that, Adam. She's very sensitive, and Edward embarrassed her greatly. You know, she's very fond of you.

ADAM. I hope she is. I'm very fond of her. But not in the least in that way, Fanny. She's a charming, dear girl, and I hope she'll soon marry someone of her own age. Even if I wanted to marry her, I'm much too old.

FANNY. You're not old, Adam.

ADAM. Too old for her. Girls ought to marry boys. That's what's the matter with America.

FANNY (*puzzled by what appears to be an abrupt change* of conversation). America?

ADAM. Yes. Why is the American child so God Awful?

FANNY (*impatiently*). I haven't the faintest idea!

ADAM. Because its father is usually about twenty years older than its mother. I don't like these one-foot-in-the-grave parents. Doreen ought to marry a chap about twenty-five—not a minute older.

FANNY. He couldn't keep her.

ADAM. Let them earn their keep and rise together.

FANNY. Adam, I want to speak to you about something else!

ADAM. What is it?

FANNY. It's about Edward and Aunt Essie. They're becoming intolerable.

ADAM. Yes. I don't care for them very much myself.

FANNY. That scene at tea this afternoon—we can't go on like that, Adam.

ADAM. No. The old woman's bad enough, but she'll probably be called home before long, though I can't believe the trumpets will sound for *her* on the other side. It's Edward I can't stand. I'm sorry, Fanny. He's your brother, of course! . . .

FANNY. Don't apologize. I can't stand him, either. Do you know, I can never remember coming into a room without seeing him with a glass of whiskey by his side. I hate drunkards. I suppose we were badly brought up. Edward's never had to do anything . . . not seriously. If you've no character, that sort of upbringing is ruinous.

ADAM. Yes-s-s, yes! What do you suggest?

FANNY. I'll get rid of them, if you'll let me. You mustn't go back on me, Adam. You know, you're too good-natured.

ADAM. I don't feel good-natured. Sometimes, I'm frightened when I think how hard I'm getting. It's this blasted money. So many people are holding out their hands to me now . . . not like that . . . (*he makes the gesture of one shaking hands*) but like that . . . (*he makes the gesture of a cupped hand in appeal*) that I see the world as a crowd of importunate beggars, all whining and snivelling and cadging, and I want to shout out "Damn your eyes, die of hunger!" I don't like myself when I feel like that.

FANNY. I quite understand. Quite. Then I have your authority to get rid of them.

ADAM. Yes . . . out of this house. I'll look after them, of course.

FANNY. Thank you. You won't be worried at all. Of course, there's one drawback to their going.

ADAM. Drawback? Can there be?

FANNY. Yes. I shall have to go, too.

ADAM. But why?

FANNY. Oh, my dear Adam, have you to be told that? I'm a widow, still young enough to be scandalized. What would be said if I were to live here . . . with you . . . alone? (ADAM, *dismayed by this, does not answer*.) It won't be easy to leave this house. I've lived in it a long time, and I love it. Arthur makes fun of its old-fashioned furniture, but I adore every stick. I like to think of Uncle Sam's father and mother, when they were first engaged, buying it . . . so young and happy. It's stood here for nearly a hundred years, Adam. This was the country when it was brought here. Now it's a suburb.

ADAM. Yes. Belfast is creeping all round it. Soon we'll be shut in. I remember when you couldn't see a single house from that window. You could walk from the gate to the top of the Holywood Hills and scarcely see a soul. Now, there are houses everywhere.

FANNY. I remember those days. How sweet the country smelt. I used to draw in my breath so that I could smell the salt air and the whin blossoms at Easter.

ADAM. Oh, yes. And the scent of hay and seaweed. Do you remember the sound of country carts coming down a loaning? Crack, crack, crack! . . .

FANNY. Weren't they lovely to look at, red and bright blue?

ADAM. Yes, yes. And the farmer calling, "Gee-up er that!" to his horse. Oh, lovely days! All gone! Motor cars, now, stinking petrol. I suppose it's because I'm getting old, but somehow the country doesn't smell so sweet as it did when I was young. Can you remember the first time you were conscious of beauty?

FANNY. Beauty? No!

ADAM. I can. I was under ten, and I'd been ill and expected to die. When I was well again, I went for a walk along a road that ran between fields and had trees on either side, not far from this house. And as I walked, I suddenly perceived how beautiful bare, black branches are. I'd known that trees in foliage are lovely. That's easy to know. All abundance is beautiful. But not until then had I realized the beauty of bareness . . . I was going to say of destitution. All the trees were leafless, and I saw them standing, dark and delicate, against a wintry sky. I was only a little boy, Fanny, and a sick little boy, but as I stood there, gazing at those bare branches, my eyes filled with tears as I thought how terrible it would have been if I had died without ever perceiving their beauty.

FANNY (*who is beginning to be bored*). How interesting! What odd thoughts children have! Of course, nature is nice. And, of course, it's very nice in Ireland. I mean, everybody knows how lovely Ireland is, though, myself, I sometimes think it's a little melancholy. All those sad and rather sombre fields. I prefer the South of France and sunshine. But Ireland *is* beautiful. That's generally admitted.

ADAM (*his mood entirely changed*). Yes, I believe its beauty is much remarked on in guide books. Hotel-keepers speak highly of it.

FANNY (*briskly and brightly*). Now, you're being

sarcastic! Well, I must go and see to things. Poor Martha, always looking after the house. Not like Mary, dreaming all day long. And how lucky for everybody that poor Martha *did* see to things.

ADAM. Yes, very lucky. I always sympathized with . . . poor Martha. She did so much and saw so little.

FANNY. She saw more than people think. But she wasn't always talking about it. You won't forget what I said, Adam?

ADAM. No. What was it?

FANNY. Well, you're going to look after Edward and Aunt Essie when they go. Will you look after us, when we've gone . . . Arthur and Doreen and me?

ADAM. But why must you go?

FANNY (*laughing a little contemptuously*). Oh, Adam! (*Then she goes out abruptly.*)

[ADAM *sits for a few moments, staring at the door through which* FANNY *has vanished. As he does so* JOHN JAMES GOURLAY *comes to the French window.*]

JOHN JAMES. Sir!

ADAM. Yes? Oh, yes, John James! What is it?

JOHN JAMES. Do you want me any more the night?

ADAM. I don't think so.

JOHN JAMES. Because there's a wee job I want to finish, an' it'll fill in the time nicely before I go home . . . if you don't want me for anythin' else.

ADAM. No, I don't want you, John James.

JOHN JAMES. Very well, sir. (*He turns to go, but* ADAM *stops him*).

ADAM. John James!

JOHN JAMES (*turning back*). Sir!

ADAM. What do you think of this marrying business?

JOHN JAMES. Next to nothin', sir!

ADAM. But you were married yourself!

JOHN JAMES. Ay!

ADAM. A long while!

JOHN JAMES. Ay. Thirty-seven years. A darned long while. An' you know, I never liked her.

ADAM. Oh! Why did you marry her, then?

JOHN JAMES. Och, why does anybody do anythin'?

Sure, we don't know why we do half the things we do. She was always on to me. If it wasn't one thing, it was another. Afore we were married, she was always sayin' men had no control of themselves. They wur the slaves of their passions, she said, and she would have it I was one. Well, sir, she riz me dandher over that, an' I up and I spoke til her. I'll bet you ten bob, I said, I could sleep with you an' not lay a han' on you. I'll bet you ten bob you couldn't, says she.

ADAM. And who won?

JOHN JAMES. Ah, she did. You're not comin' out again?

ADAM. No.

JOHN JAMES. Then I'll bid you good-night. (*He turns away*).

ADAM. Good-night.

JOHN JAMES (*at the window*). You know, sometimes I fancy she led me on.

ADAM. I wouldn't be surprised.

[JOHN JAMES *goes out, and the act ends.*

ACT III

We are again in the morning-room, a few days later. The time is Saturday mid-morning. EDWARD *is seated in an arm-chair, contemplating the ceiling. A decanter of whiskey and a syphon of soda stand on a small table by his side. He has a full glass in his hand.* AUNT ESSIE *is seated near him, reading the ' Belfast News-Letter.' She puts the paper down on her lap for a moment, while she wipes her spectacles.* EDWARD *takes a swig of the whiskey, and then puts the glass on the table.*

EDWARD. Have you finished with the paper?

MRS. CORKEN (*adjusting her glasses on her nose*). No.

EDWARD (*irritably*). You must be reading everything in it twice. Give me the inside.

MRS. CORKEN (*picking up the paper again*). No.

EDWARD. Well, give me the outside, then.

MRS. CORKEN. I can't bear a paper in pieces. You'll have to wait.

EDWARD. You're the contrariest old woman I ever met. What are you reading anyway?

MRS. CORKEN. The births, deaths and marriages. I don't know one of the people that's got married or had children, but I know three that's dead, and two of them are younger nor I am. That's a great satisfaction to me.

EDWARD. I don't see why I should have to wait for the paper 'til you've studied the tables of mortality.

MRS. CORKEN. I'm not studying them. I'm just getting satisfaction out of them.

EDWARD. I can't understand you. You seem to rejoice in other people's death. What good will it do you to survive all your friends and acquaintances. It's no fun to be left alone in a world of young that hasn't a ha'pporth of understanding or sympathy for you, and wishes to God you were dead !

MRS. CORKEN. You're a very melancholy man, Edward.

74

It's all the drink you take. Why don't you buy a paper of your own?

EDWARD. What would be the sense of that when there's one comes in the house? And it isn't yours, anyway! It's Adam's.

MRS. CORKEN. Ring that bell by the side of you.

EDWARD. What for?

MRS. CORKEN (*firmly*). Ring it! (*He does so.*) Nobody'll do anything for you in this house without you explaining to them in words of three letters why you want it done. Isn't it enough that a body wants a thing without them having to go into every mortal detail? Ring again, will you?

EDWARD. Och, give them time to get here.

MRS. CORKEN. That's not the way to work at all. Make them hurry, whatever it's for. Go on. Ring.

EDWARD (*ringing again*). Have you said any more to Adam about the money?

MRS. CORKEN. I've never stopped saying something about it. It's my belief that woman Fanny—I never liked her, God forgive me—is scheming against us. She'll have the half of the fortune, or mebbe the whole of it, if we don't watch out. It's about time you and me got together for our own good.

EDWARD. I'm ready for anything that'll make me safe and secure.   [KATE *enters.*

KATE. Were you ringin'?

MRS. CORKEN. Was I ringing? Did you ever hear the like, and me with my fingers nearly worn to the bone ringing? Doesn't any person in this house answer a bell the first time it's rung?

KATE. I was upstairs, and Mary's busy. We can't be in two places at once.

MRS. CORKEN. You don't try.

KATE. Well, what do you want?

MRS. CORKEN (*indicating the French window*). Shut that door, will you. There's a draught.

KATE (*as she shuts it*). Is that all you rung for?

MRS. CORKEN. Uh-huh!

KATE. Draggin' me from the top of the house for that, an' the pair of you well able to shut the door yourselves.

EDWARD. I didn't know she wanted it shut. You never told me you wanted it shut. (*Takes up his glass again.*) I'd 'a' shut it if you'd asked me. (*He drains the glass.*)

MRS. CORKEN. What's servants for? I wasn't brought up to do for myself what a servant could do. You're getting too far above yourself, Kate. It's that legacy you were left. What would the like of you do if the like of us didn't find work for you?

KATE. Och, we'd do well enough. Better, mebbe.

MRS. CORKEN. The world doesn't know itself these days. Servants are like lords. Let me tell you this, my lady, one of these days, when everybody has labour-saving devices, people like us'll be able to do without servants altogether, and then where'll you be?

KATE. In heaven, I hope.

MRS. CORKEN. Ah, dear, dear, dear! Things aren't what they used to be. Nothing like it. In my young days, a serving girl worked from dawn 'til dark, and thought herself lucky if she got five shillings a week and her keep. But now, servants give their orders, and we take them. Ha!

KATE. Is there anything else you want?

MRS. CORKEN. Clean against the Scripture. That's what it is. Clean against the Scripture. Servants, be obedient to your masters. St. Paul himself said it! . . .

KATE. Do you want anything else while I'm here.

MRS. CORKEN. I'll ring if I do.

EDWARD (*as he pours himself out another drink*). Is there a nice dinner the night, Kate?

KATE. There's always a nice dinner, Mr. Edward.

EDWARD. Well, what is there?

KATE. Ah, wait an' see. I wouldn't like to deprive you of the pleasure of a surprise.

EDWARD. That meat last night was a bit underdone for me. I like it well done.

KATE. Some likes it rare an' some likes it red.

MRS. CORKEN. I like it red. And my taste has as much right to be considered as yours, Edward.

EDWARD. I'm not complaining, I'm not complaining. All I said is that I like my meat well done. That's all. If the rest of you want it underdone, all right, have it underdone. But can't I just say I like it well done? There's no harm in just saying a thing, is there?

MRS. CORKEN. Yes. Plenty.

EDWARD. Why can't we all have what we want? That's what I'd like to know.

[FANNY *enters.*

FANNY. What are you doing upstairs, Kate?

KATE. Changin' rooms.

FANNY. What rooms?

KATE. Mrs. Corken's an' the master's.

FANNY. Who told you to change them?

KATE. He did.

MRS. CORKEN. Yes. I arranged it with Adam. I don't like the room I'm in, and he doesn't mind where he sleeps.

FANNY. But that's the master's room.

KATE. I said so. It's always been the master's room. Sir Sam slept there, after his parents, all the years of his life.

FANNY. You take a great deal on yourself, Aunt Essie.

MRS. CORKEN. Oh, indeed! And who gave you the right to lay down the law?

FANNY. I'm in charge of this house. I looked after it for Uncle Sam, and I'm looking after it for Adam. Please don't give orders here without my consent.

MRS. CORKEN. *Your* consent! . . .

FANNY (*dismissing* KATE). All right, Kate. (*Exit* KATE.) And please don't shout, Aunt Essie. I'm not deaf.

MRS. CORKEN. You have a face of brass, Fanny. That's what you have. A face of brass! . . .

FANNY. You'll stay in your present room . . . while you're here. I'll tell Kate to put your things back.

[*She goes towards the door as she speaks.*

MRS. CORKEN. You'll do no such thing!

FANNY (*opening the door*). Kate. Kate!

KATE (*outside*). Yes, mem!

FANNY. Come here a moment! (*She returns to the centre of the room.*) You're both utterly selfish. (*To* EDWARD.) Can't you stop swilling?

EDWARD. Why should I? I like it. The trouble with you, Fanny, is you can't leave well alone. Let things be.

FANNY. And a nice state they'd be in if I did. (KATE

enters.) Oh, Kate, put Mrs. Corken's things back in her room.

KATE. It was Mr. Adam bid me change them!

FANNY. I'll answer for that.

KATE. Very well, mem.

FANNY. Oh, and Kate, don't make any alterations until you've consulted me.

KATE (*a little doubtfully*). No, mem! [*Exit.*

FANNY. You understand, Aunt Essie, I hope. In future, you give no orders in this house without my consent.

MRS. CORKEN. Don't Adam's orders count, then?

FANNY. He lets himself be imposed on.

EDWARD (*reaching for the News Letter which has been lying unread on* AUNT ESSIE'S *lap ever since* FANNY'S *entrance*). As you're not reading the paper, I'll just take a look at it.

MRS. CORKEN (*snatching it from him*). You'll do no such thing! (*To* FANNY.) Of course, I'm a poor old woman and need expect no deference from anybody. But this was my brother's house, and I have more right to give orders in it nor any other person, and as long as God spares me, I'll stand up for my rights. I feel affronted to be spoken to like that before a servant. Affronted—that's what I feel. But we know well what your object is. Me and Edward here, poor drunkard though he is, we know well what you're up to. Mistress of this house—that's what you want to be! And we're to be turned out ... to starve, mebbe! ...

FANNY. Don't be foolish, Aunt Essie.

MRS. CORKEN. But you'll never prosper, Fanny, never in this world, if you dishonour them that are older nor you. The Bible says a thankless child is worse nor a serpent's tooth. Now, don't tell me that's in Shakespeare. Every time I quote the Bible, somebody tells me Shakespeare wrote it. You'd ne'er think that man wrote anything.

EDWARD. You're taking one another up too sharp. Why can't you both do the same as I do: take whatever comes your way without fuss or botheration? We're very nicely placed here, and I think the wise thing is to do as little as possible to disturb things. Anyway, I'm well content.

FANNY. But we're not content with you, Edward.

EDWARD (*who doesn't like her tone at all*). Oh!

FANNY. Not at all content! It's about time you went back to your rooms.

EDWARD. But I gave them up long ago.

FANNY. Well, take them on again. You've been here long enough.

MRS. CORKEN. Didn't I tell you what it would be? Putting us out now.

FANNY. Adam's under no obligation to keep you, Edward.

EDWARD. I think he is. He has money that morally belongs to me. And, anyway, I've been kept the whole of my life.

MRS. CORKEN. The more shame to you.

EDWARD. So have you.

MRS. CORKEN. I'm a woman. You're a man.

EDWARD. Well, now we've got equality of the sexes, it's the same for you as it is for us.

MRS. CORKEN. I never asked for equality. I don't believe in it, and I don't want it. All I ask is to be maintained in the style I'm accustomed to! . . .

FANNY. The sooner you're out of this house, Edward, the better. I'll tell Kate to have your things packed this afternoon.

EDWARD. You needn't bother. I'm not shifting myself. (*Helping himself to a long swig.*) I think I know a good thing when I see it.

FANNY. You're leaving this afternoon, Edward. Your suitcases will be in the hall at half-past two. And with whiskey the price it is, you might buy your own.

EDWARD. With whiskey the price it is, that would be a damned foolish thing to do. What authority have you to put me out?

[ADAM *enters from the garden.*

FANNY. Every authority. Adam will tell you himself what it is.

ADAM. What's that?

FANNY. I'm making some changes, Adam. I'm putting Aunt Essie back in her room and you in yours.

ADAM. Oh, but I agreed to let her have mine.

MRS. CORKEN. There you are, you see!

FANNY. Well, I've told her she can't have it. You are the master of this house, and must sleep in the master's room. I've told Edward it's time he went back to his lodgings.

EDWARD. Yes, Adam, I've been turned out. I'm fifty-three years of age, and I'm being cast on the world by my own relations. Is that your will?

ADAM. You're not being exactly cast on the world, Edward, but you've been here rather a long time, haven't you?

EDWARD. If I've outstayed my welcome! . . .

ADAM. I don't remember any welcome. My recollection is that you came to tea . . . and remained.

EDWARD. No one will ever be able to say that I stayed where I wasn't wanted. I'll go this minute.

ADAM. Oh, stay to lunch.

EDWARD. No, I'll go now. I couldn't eat a morsel of food in this house after being told to go. It would choke me.

[*He starts towards the door, but, remembering his whiskey and soda, turns back and drains the glass. Then he stalks across the room.*]

MRS. CORKEN. I suppose I'll be the next to be flung on the world.

EDWARD (*at the door*). I'm practically destitute. What'll become of me?

FANNY. Go to a Labour Exchange and ask for work.

EDWARD (*appalled*). Work! At my age! Me that's never done a hand's turn in my life. Have you no Christian feeling, Fanny?

MRS. CORKEN. I can't begin working now.

ADAM. I think, Aunt Essie, you'll be much happier elsewhere. Of course, I shall provide for you. Both of you.

MRS. CORKEN. How much?

FANNY. A reasonable amount.

MRS. CORKEN. I'm not asking you. How much, Adam?

ADAM. As Fanny says, a reasonable sum.

EDWARD. But what she'd call reasonable and what *we'd* call reasonable are two different things.

ADAM. I don't know how long you're likely to live, Edward, but I'll see you through what's left of your life.

EDWARD.   Well, that doesn't sound so bad.   I could manage on twelve pounds a week.

FANNY.   Twelve pounds a month 'ud be more like it.

EDWARD.   I wouldn't be married to you for a mint of money.   Look out for yourself, Adam.   That woman has her eye on you.

MRS. CORKEN.   That's the truest word you ever spoke in your life, Edward.   (*To Adam.*)   She'll have you like a fly on a pin! . . .

ADAM.   If you and Edward were to live together, aunt, you could manage very comfortably.

MRS. CORKEN.   Me live with him!   He'd drink me out of hearth and home.

EDWARD.   I wouldn't live with her for twice the money. She'd have me distracted mad in a month.   Did you say I could stay 'til lunch?

ADAM.   Yes!   Yes!   Do.

EDWARD.   If the food's here, there's no sense in me going elsewhere for it.

[*He comes into the room as if he were about to resume his seat, but* FANNY *halts him.*]

FANNY.   You can be doing your packing now.

EDWARD.   Oh, ay, ay!   I suppose so.   It would be more convenient to move on Monday.   The week-end, you know.   (*This suggestion is received in silence.*)   Oh, well!

[*And out he goes.*

MRS. CORKEN.   That's a very poor creature, that!   Not an inch of backbone in his body.   He'll die a fearful death. Am I to go the day or when?

ADAM.   There's no hurry.

FANNY.   I've found very nice rooms for you, Aunt Essie! . . .

MRS. CORKEN.   You've found me rooms!

FANNY.   They're on the Malone Road, near the University.   A very nice neighbourhood! . . .

MRS. CORKEN.   I don't like the Malone Road.   I don't want to be next or near the University.   Students here and students there, skylarking about and making uproars and rags.   I'd rather be somewhere near-hand . . . like The Knock, mebbe, or Dundela! . . .

FANNY.   The rooms I've got you are very good indeed.

F

They're kept by the widow of a Presbyterian minister! . . .

MRS. CORKEN. But I'm an Episcopalian.

FANNY. I've engaged them for you.

MRS. CORKEN (*rising in her wrath*). You've engaged them for me. Without a word or a syllable to me.

FANNY. I told Mrs. Robb you'd arrive this evening in time for tea.

> [*This is too much for* AUNT ESSIE *who, after gazing incredulously at* FANNY, *sinks back in her seat and dissolves into tears. When her face is seen again, it appears suddenly to have become senile. The old woman is down and out at last.*]

MRS. CORKEN. My own brother's house . . . turned out of my own brother's house . . . and no place but strange lodgings to go to . . . where nobody knows me or wants me . . . an old woman . . . an old, old woman! . . . Aw-w-w!

> [*She has risen and is making her way almost blindly out of the room. She leaves the door open, and the sound of her sobbing can be heard until* ADAM *shuts the door. He comes into the room. Both he and* FANNY *are silent for a moment.*]

ADAM. You are very hard on her, Fanny.

FANNY. It's no use being soft. They're both old and useless and in the way. The sooner they go, the better.

ADAM. I wonder if any one will ever say that about us?

FANNY. I daresay. We shall deserve it if we give them an excuse for saying it.

ADAM. It isn't their fault that they're what they are. They were reared to that.

FANNY. My dear Adam, if we start looking for the source of blame, we'll go back to the beginning of time. People have some responsibility for themselves. If their standard is low, it's because they've lowered it. I hate all this stuff Arthur talks about victims of environment. I'm not the victim of my environment. I'm the master of it. If I let circumstances get the better of me, I deserve all I get.

ADAM. In theory, I'm with you. I'm a follower of Pelagius, Fanny.

FANNY. Who?

ADAM. Pelagius. A distinguished Ulsterman who lived in the time of St. Augustine. That Arab, I regret to say got the better of him, but the world would have been a happier place if Pelagius had got the better of Augustine. He believed that we can lift ourselves up if we want to. That, broadly speaking, and in theory, is my own belief. " If we ought," said Pelagius, " we can." But I'm not so rigorous a Pelagian as you, Fanny.

FANNY. I never heard of him until this minute.

ADAM. You can be influenced by a man without ever having heard of him. As I say, I'm not so rigorous a Pelagian as you are. Neither was he. Followers are usually more fanatical than their leaders. That's a pity! I feel, and Pelagius felt, that systems ought not to be carried to excess. He was too tolerant a man . . . an Ulsterman, of course . . . and might have overcome Augustine if he had been as oppressive as the Arab. But with his belief, oppression was impossible. He had to be tolerant or illogical, and he preferred to be tolerant. I sometimes wish that when he disappeared from Palestine and Lydda, he had come back to Ireland and spread his tolerant, manly mind among his own people. Your trouble, Fanny, is that you believe in his theory, but not in his practice. Like Pelagius, like me, you believe that we can lift ourselves up, but, unlike Pelagius and me, you despise those who don't. I feel, Fanny, that the Almighty is so wealthy that he can afford to waste a little. Aunt Essie and Edward are little bits of waste. Need we feel indignant with the chippings because they aren't the statue?

FANNY. No, but the chippings must be swept away.

ADAM. You have all the logic. Perhaps Pelagius was wise to disappear.

FANNY. Have you thought about . . . me?

ADAM. I'm always thinking of you.

FANNY. Listen, Adam! Our position is an unusual one, and it requires plain statements. I can't stay in this house alone with you. I'm still, comparatively speaking, a young woman.

ADAM. Of course, you are. No one can think of you as anything else.

FANNY. Flattery makes no impression on me. Facts do.

I'm the mother of a grown-up son and daughter. They're my main facts. All the same, I'm still, as women go, a young woman. And I'm living in this house with you.

ADAM. You lived here with Uncle Sam! . . .

FANNY. He was an old man. We're about the same age. And people say things.

ADAM. Does it matter to us what they say?

FANNY. It matters to me. I'm a conventional woman, and I like to be respected by my neighbours. It wounds me to think that people are making remarks about me that are unpleasant.

ADAM. Are they?

FANNY. Yes.

ADAM. Who are they?

FANNY. Oh, nobody makes remarks straight at me, but I hear hints and whispers. They'll become public clamour now that Aunt Essie and Edward are going! . . .

ADAM. In that case, ask them to stay!

FANNY. No, Adam, for your sake, they must go. And I must go, for my own sake . . . unless! . . .

ADAM. Unless what?

FANNY. You and I are no longer romantic, Adam, and we can face facts realistically. I mean, we can take a more detached and reasonable view of . . . marriage, say, than Doreen or even Arthur. It's possible for people of our age to come to . . . an arrangement! . . .

ADAM. What exactly are you proposing, Fanny?

FANNY. I'm being talked about. I don't like being talked about. I must either leave this house or remain under very different conditions.

ADAM. Do you mean that I should marry you?

FANNY. Yes.

ADAM (*rising in his astonishment*). But, my dear Fanny! . . .

FANNY. Sit down. We must discuss this calmly.

ADAM (*relapsing into his seat*). I'm not used to receiving proposals of marriage.

FANNY. I'm not used to making them. We'd better make allowance for our inexperience. I had a right to expect Uncle Sam to leave most of his fortune to me.

ADAM. He evidently didn't think so. Personally, I think he should have left it to Jenny.

FANNY. I'm not interested in Miss Conn. Men have sides to their lives which I, as a virtuous woman, prefer not to know. I take an old-fashioned attitude towards irregular relations . . . and their results. They are wrong, and should be discouraged. That's where I disagree with Arthur. If his opinions were to prevail, our whole moral code would founder. I'm afraid I sound as if I were lecturing you ! . . .

ADAM. Go on, I'm interested.

FANNY. In my experience, Adam, when you tamper with a system, no matter how slightly, you do harm that will spread until you have destroyed the entire system. Treat a bastard as if it were a legitimate child, and how long will marriage last ? I don't doubt that Miss Conn is an admirable woman, but she is a bastard, and must suffer for her misfortune.

ADAM. But it isn't her fault.

FANNY. It isn't the fault of a blind man that he's blind, but he has to bear it.

ADAM. Would you refuse to cure the blind man even if his blindness were his own fault?

FANNY. I would, if the cure endangered other people's sight. But that's not what I wanted to say. You agree, don't you, that I had a right to expect this property? Morally, it's mine. Morally, no one has less right to it than you.

ADAM. I'm not so sure of that now, but when I was, I wanted to share the fortune with you. You wouldn't hear of that.

FANNY. Like Miss Conn, I'm against division. Split money is no good to anybody. It just enables people to waste themselves. If you marry me, I shall receive what's due to me, the money will be kept intact, and you'll be no worse off than you are. I shall make you a good wife.

ADAM. I'm sure you will. I'm not sure that you won't be too good a wife.

FANNY. That's intellectual wit, I suppose. I don't think much of it. I've heard a lot of that sort of stuff from Arthur. It's all right in undergraduates, but not in adult men.

ADAM. Fanny, I'm not trying to be funny ! . . .

FANNY. As I say, I shall make you a good wife. I run this house efficiently. I'm not bad looking! . . .

ADAM. You're very handsome.

FANNY. I dress well. I know how to hold myself in company. I respect myself and I shall respect my husband.

ADAM. Yes, you're very satisfactory, Fanny, and if you require a testimonial at any time, I'll give you one. But you have one serious defect from my point of view.

FANNY. What's that?

ADAM. You don't love me, and I don't love you.

FANNY. At our age, that's not a defect, it's an advantage.

ADAM. I don't think so.

FANNY. We are two middle-aged people, making an arrangement about life. Don't let us mix it up with emotion. Any number of people in the world marry without the slightest affection for each other. They make an arrangement to live together and produce children. I've not noticed that such marriages are less happy or successful than those which . . . are made in heaven. I married Willie for love, and our marriage was a complete failure.

ADAM. Your argument is irrefutable, Fanny, but I'm in favour of love.

FANNY. All the same, I ask you to marry me.

ADAM. But I don't want to marry you.

FANNY. Why? You admit I'm attractive.

ADAM. Yes, very!

FANNY. Willie found me very satisfactory . . . in every way.

ADAM. I'm not Willie, and I mightn't find you satisfactory at all. You see, Fanny, I haven't that clamant desire for you that a man ought to feel for the woman he wants to marry. I'm really very romantic, and I want to possess and be possessed by my wife, and to feel myself unable to live without her. I can live without you quite easily.

FANNY. Well, that's frank.

ADAM. I *am* frank . . . with *you*. If I loved you, I would probably lie like a lawyer to save you from anxiety and distress. I'd cheat for you, steal for you, kill for you. I'm as romantic as that. But as I don't love you, the entire Decalogue is perfectly safe. You'd better let me make you an allowance. It'll be substantial. I don't really want much myself.

FANNY. You don't want me.

ADAM. I shall be glad if you'll stay here, just as you did in Sir Sam's day! . . .

FANNY. But you don't want me.

ADAM. No.

FANNY. I feel humiliated.

ADAM. Why? We're two middle-aged people, calmly discussing a business proposal. One of us doesn't like it. That's all.

FANNY. That isn't all. Your life's insufficient. That's why your books are unpopular. People won't read them because they know in their hearts you don't know what you're talking about. You don't even know the little bit of life you call your own. You walk round your own feelings, though they don't amount to much, and when you've finished, you're as ignorant as when you started. I know very little about authors and artists, Adam, but I do know this much, there's no genius in a man who hasn't any exuberance or excess. There's never been a great man who wasn't always spilling over. You've never spilt over in your life. You've a ha'penny mind, Adam, like a peasant.

ADAM. Peasant! Me?

FANNY. Yes. You want to be let alone, to be a little unattached person, remote from everybody and everything but your own people and your own affairs. What's that but greedy self-absorption? Poor ignorant Paddy, incompetently dibbling in a little field, and producing, year after year, the same dull crop of little potatoes, until at last the starved field refuses to produce any more, and there's a famine! I could widen your life, Adam, and make you love me.

ADAM. I don't want it widened. I like a little life.

[ARTHUR *enters.*

ARTHUR. Hillo. Having a pow-wow.

[FANNY *is still for a moment, then she hurries out of the room.*]

ARTHUR. What's the matter with mother?

ADAM. I don't think there's anything the matter with her. But there's something the matter with me.

ARTHUR. Well, why don't you send for a doctor?

ADAM. I think I will.

ARTHUR. I didn't interrupt anything, did I?

ADAM. Broadly speaking, Arthur, you interrupt everything.

ARTHUR. Nobody takes me seriously, and I ought to be taken seriously. I've a good mind to clear out. I'm belittled by the entire family.

ADAM. You're too clever, my boy, much, much too clever. You've read a lot, but you know nothing, and you're suffering from a very common complaint.

ARTHUR. Oh! What's that?

ADAM. Intestinal destitution. You've no guts. (*He rings the bell.*)

ARTHUR. I'd like to have a good talk with you, Adam. About fundamentals. Nobody in this house ever talks about fundamentals.

ADAM. You're not proposing to have it now, are you?

ARTHUR. Why not? I'm always ready to have a good talk . . . a real talk . . . about fundamentals . . . now to-morrow, next week, any time. The truth is, Adam, there's no real politics in this country. Either you're for a republic or you're against it, and that's all. There hasn't been any real political policy in this country since St. Patrick set about the snakes.

ADAM. You're too ready to discuss things, Arthur. Fundamentals are not to be talked about at any time! They wouldn't be fundamentals if they were. You have to prepare yourself for them, to be in the mood and the mind. Religious people are quite right when they begin their deliberations with prayer. We ought to calm our minds and put ourselves in tune with greatness before we discuss it. I have an old-fashioned belief in God, which I'm sure you will think contemptible! . . .

ARTHUR. Oh! I wouldn't say that. I'm ready to discuss divinity with anybody.

ADAM. Not now, Arthur. You see, I'm not calm enough for that.

ARTHUR. That's mother, of course. For a quiet woman, she's extraordinarily disturbing. But you and I ! . . .

[KATE *enters.*

ADAM. Excuse me, Arthur. Oh, Kate, will you tell McIlveen to bring the car round to the door at once. I want him to deliver a letter for me. I'll have it ready by the time he comes to the door.

KATE. Very good, sir! [*Exit.*

ADAM. Sorry, Arthur. A cosy conversation about the Almighty would, I am sure, be very beneficial to me, but I shall have to leave it until another time.

[*He goes out, leaving* ARTHUR *abashed.* DOREEN
enters from the garden.]

DOREEN. Nobody here?

ARTHUR. Yes, I am.

DOREEN. Who went out just now?

ARTHUR. Adam. He'd been jawing with mother, and they're both as shirty as hell.

DOREEN. What's mother up to?

ARTHUR. Ask me another. I don't know. I thought she was trying to marry you to Adam. Was she?

DOREEN. You don't have to try to marry me to people.

ARTHUR. Well, are you going to marry him?

DOREEN. Mind your own business.

ARTHUR. It is my business. My future's at stake.

DOREEN (*scornfully*). *Your* future?

ARTHUR. Yes, my future. I have one. This country's in a frightful state. It needs a fresh mind. Personally, I don't think there's any hope for Ireland until there's been six or seven first-class funerals. We must get rid of all the people who were " out " in 1916, and all the people who were " out " at the Boyne. It's time I was in parliament, and I shall need money for it.

DOREEN. If I marry Adam, I won't let him waste a penny on you, Master Arthur. I shall need all he has.

ARTHUR. He's got to provide for us, you know.

DOREEN. You can provide for yourself. If you want a future, you must make it. But I may as well tell you, Adam doesn't intend to marry me.

ARTHUR. Have you asked him?

DOREEN. No, of course I haven't asked him. But I can tell. He treats me as if I were a child. I've half a mind to go to London.

ARTHUR. What for?

DOREEN. Oh, just for something to do. Jenny Conn said I ought to take a job.

ARTHUR. Well, why don't you? Lead your own life.

[FANNY *enters.*

DOREEN. Oh, hillo, mother!

FANNY. I thought Adam was here.

ARTHUR. He was, but he went out soon after you did. He's sending a message to somebody.

FANNY. Who to?

ARTHUR. He didn't say.

FANNY. Well, if he comes back, you two can go out. I want to talk to him privately.

ARTHUR. Righto!

FANNY. What have you been doing, Doreen?

DOREEN. Oh, knocking around. Mother, will you let me go to London?

FANNY. London! By yourself?

DOREEN. Yes.

FANNY. But, my dear, what for?

DOREEN. I want to do something. I'm tired of this lolling around! . . .

FANNY. Do what?

DOREEN. I don't know. Something.

ARTHUR. She wants to lead her own life.

FANNY. Have you been suggesting that to her?

ARTHUR. No, but that's what she wants.

DOREEN. I think I ought to go away from home, mother.

FANNY. From me?

DOREEN. Well, yes. I'd like to have rooms or a flat or something . . . a place of my own.

FANNY. Are you serious?

DOREEN. Yes, mother.

FANNY. Do you mean you want to leave me . . . to go off by yourself . . . to London?

DOREEN. Yes.

FANNY. But it's absurd, darling!

DOREEN. I don't see anything absurd about it. It's natural, isn't it? The young always leave the old.

ARTHUR. Every bird makes its own nest.

FANNY. Can either of you make a nest?

DOREEN. We've got to try some time, mother. We'll never learn to make it if we stay here . . . with you.

FANNY. This is foolish talk. Every bird that makes its own nest finds its own worms. Are you going to find yours? Or am I to find them for you?

DOREEN. Well, of course, I should expect an allowance.

FANNY. Exactly. And that's what you call leading your own life? Why, you couldn't earn fifteen shillings a week.

DOREEN. Well, whose fault is that? It isn't much credit to you, mother, that you've spent a lot of money on my education and then tell me I'm not fit to earn fifteen shillings a week.

ARTHUR. A more damning verdict of capitalistic civilization than that, I have never heard.

FANNY. One of these days, Arthur, you will terrify yourself by growing up. (*To* DOREEN.) You can't go to London or anywhere else by yourself. Your place is with me.

DOREEN. I shouldn't want very much, mother!

FANNY. How much?

DOREEN. Well, enough to live on . . . decently, I mean.

FANNY. And how much is that?

DOREEN. I don't know.

FANNY. I thought you didn't.

ARTHUR. You couldn't do it under two hundred a year.

FANNY. Do you ever stop to think how you're living now, how I've managed to keep you since your father died? Not you! You take it all for granted. This is your right . . . though you've done nothing to earn it. I've schemed and schemed for you, humiliating myself sometimes so that you might be secure. If I hadn't worked as I have, Arthur, do you suppose you'd ever had seen Eton or Oxford? Never in this world. Your father was a weak man, with no will or work in him, and he died without a penny. I made Uncle Sam keep us. I didn't like him, and he didn't like me, but I forced his hand and I kept it forced for your sakes. I may have been a foolish woman, but I did the best I could.

ARTHUR. We're not blaming you, mother.

FANNY (*bitterly*). Thank you, Arthur.

ARTHUR. Of course, I'm against all these middle-class, bourgeois ideas. Politically, I'm a proletarian.

DOREEN. Would you just look at the horny-handed son of toil!

ARTHUR. Shut up, you. Being funny about fundamentals isn't funny. I think your struggle, mother, was a waste of effort, but I realize that it was a struggle, and although I don't respect the purpose, I do respect the effort. Your whole view of life, of course, is all wrong. The day for this sort of thing is over. (*He indicates the room with a sweep of his hand.*) We're starting a new world! . . .

FANNY. Who are " we "?

ARTHUR. My generation, of course.

FANNY. Do you suppose nobody ever thought of starting anything until you were born? There were hare-brained people before your day.

ARTHUR. Insult! Insult! Always insult. Listen, mother, I know as well as you do that reform is not new. But let me tell you that what we want now is not reform, but regeneration. We want a new world, not an old world done up, and I'm all for getting rid of junk. I want a complete break with the past. I want to go back to the beginning and start again! . . .

FANNY. And do you think that's never been done before? Didn't God Himself try to make a new world, and didn't He fail?

ARTHUR. When?

FANNY. Is that all Oxford did for you? The world, my dear Arthur, was so desperately wicked that God destroyed it by flood. He took four men and four women and separated them from the rest of mankind in the hope that when He had drowned all the wicked, He could begin a new world. If ever a man had a chance to start with every advantage, Noah was the man. He stepped into a wet and empty earth, master of all he surveyed, but he hadn't been out of the Ark five minutes before his son, Ham, found him dead drunk! . . .

ARTHUR. Yes, but he used old stuff to start his new world.

FANNY. What other stuff had he? There was no new life created in the Ark. You must make your new world out of old stuff. There isn't any other. As for you,

Doreen, you'll stay here . . . with me. I'm your mother.
I have a right to your love and obedience.

DOREEN.   You can't get love and obedience by right,
mother. They happen.

FANNY.   Don't you love me?

DOREEN.   Yes, but you're very bossy. I'd love you more
if you weren't always asking me to love you.

FANNY.   That's the cruellest thing that's ever been said
to me. (EDWARD *enters*.) Have you packed, Edward?

EDWARD.   Oh, ah, well, not what you could call
packed ! . . .

FANNY.   Well, go and finish, then.

EDWARD (*blustering*).   Look here, Fanny ! . . .

FANNY.   Don't argue, Edward. I know very well what
your game is. You think if you spin things out long
enough, Adam'll relent and let you stay. Well, you think
wrong ! You're going out of this house this afternoon.

EDWARD.   My God Almighty, what a sister ! (ADAM
enters.) Is it your will, Adam, that I'm thrown out at a
minute's notice?

ADAM.   Yes, it's my will.

EDWARD.   In that case, then ! . . . (*He turns, a bit dazed,
to go out, but stands in the middle of the room, almost
muttering to himself, for a few moments*.) The world's
not itself. The world's *not* itself. Everything's through
other. Relations barging one another, and back-chatting,
and running one another down as if they were strangers !
(*He drifts out*.)

ADAM.   I've sent for Jenny !

FANNY.   Oh ! Why?

ADAM.   We must make a final settlement now.
McIlveen's gone to fetch her.

ARTHUR.   I suppose it isn't any use my saying anything?

ADAM.   No, not a bit. Your destiny, Arthur, is to be a
lecturer on English literature at a provincial university . . .
a cross lecturer . . . the sort that belittles and derides.
You'll die in the conviction that if the world had only
listened to you, all its misfortunes would have been averted.
That will be your last self-deception.

DOREEN.   And what will I do?

ADAM.   You'll have to settle your own life, my dear.
You're too young to have it settled for you.

ARTHUR. I had planned my life! . . .

ADAM. That was your first mistake. You didn't know enough about your life to be able to plan it. Nobody does.

ARTHUR. Nobody listens to me. Nobody. But I'll make them listen to me. You wait. Just you wait. I'll make 'em listen to me! . . .

[*And with a forcible feeble air of resolution, he goes into the garden.*]

ADAM (*calling after him*). Don't go far, Arthur. I shall want you here when Jenny comes.

ARTHUR (*off*). Oh, all right!

DOREEN. I wish I were like Jenny.

ADAM. It's weak to want to be like other people. Be like yourself.

FANNY. I want to talk to Adam, Doreen! . . .

ADAM (*as* DOREEN *goes towards the door*). Don't go, Doreen! Your mother and I have nothing to say to each other that you can't hear.

FANNY. But, Adam! . . .

ADAM. I've made my mind up, Fanny. All this must end.

FANNY. End?

ADAM. Yes.

FANNY. But things can't end. They go on and on! . . .

ADAM. I know. But they can go on differently.

[KATE *enters.*

KATE. Sir, did you say there'd be seven 'til lunch?

ADAM. Yes, Kate. Miss Conn! . . .

KATE. That's who it is. I couldn't count more'n six. Will you want wine served, sir?

ADAM (*lightheartedly*). Yes, Kate, I think we will. The best wine we have.

KATE. There's a very nice Burgundy, sir. Sir Sam bought it at a sale, and was very partial to it, very partial to it. He was a great man for a glass of good wine. He'd hold it up forenenst him, and look at the light shinin' through it. (*She listens.*) Is that the car come back?

ADAM. I think so. Tell Mrs. Corken and Mr. Scantlebury I want them here.

KATE. Very good, sir. Will I bring in any rereshments?

ADAM. Not to-day, Kate.

KATE. Very good, sir. [*She goes out.*

ADAM (*to* DOREEN). Find Arthur. (DOREEN *goes into the garden.*)

FANNY. What are you going to do, Adam?

ADAM. In a moment.

FANNY. Don't do anything rash!

ADAM. I won't. [KATE *enters.*

KATE. Miss Lepper! [JENNY *enters.*

ADAM. Come in, Jenny. (*To* KATE.) Have you told Mrs. Corken . . . ?

KATE. I have, sir. They're comin'. [*She goes out.*

JENNY. Why did you send for me, Adam?

ADAM. Oh, my dear, why didn't I send for you before? [DOREEN *enters.*

DOREEN. Arthur's coming up the drive. Hillo, Jenny.

[MRS. CORKEN, *followed by* EDWARD, *enters.*

MRS. CORKEN. I hear you want me?

ADAM. Yes, Aunt Essie. Sit down, will you?

EDWARD. Have you changed your mind about us going?

ADAM. No. Sit down, Edward.

EDWARD (*as he seats himself, to* JENNY). Oh, you're here! . . .

JENNY. Yes, I'm here. You'll forgive me for breathing the same air as yourself.

EDWARD. Not funny! Not funny! There's very little these times that is funny! I mind when a man could be sure of one good laugh a day. Now, he's lucky if he gets one a month. [ARTHUR *enters.*

ADAM. Ah, now we're all here. Sit down, Arthur. (ARTHUR *does so.*) I'm going to tell you what I've made up my mind to do.

FANNY. You're not dividing the money, Adam?

ADAM. No. No, I'm not dividing it. It isn't mine to divide.

FANNY. Not yours?

EDWARD. Have you found a flaw in the will, then?

ADAM. No, there's nothing the matter with the will. It's absolutely watertight. The money's mine in the eyes of the law, but it's not mine in my eyes. I've felt that strongly since the beginning. My first instinct was to share it with you, but Jenny here . . . and you, too, Fanny . . . persuaded me not to divide it.

JENNY. Good!

ADAM. So, I'm going to do what ought to have been done by Sir Sam himself . . . give it to his child.

OMNES. What! Give it to who? Give it to Jenny!

JENNY. Did you say *me?*

ADAM. Yes.

FANNY. All of it?

ADAM. Yes, every penny. You see, Jenny, he left you to me to deal with. That was a funny bequest . . . for what could I do with you?

JENNY. I could tell you! . . .

ADAM. Oh! What?

JENNY. Not now. Some other time.

MRS. CORKEN. What happens to us?

ADAM. You must ask Jenny. It's her money. I shall ask Mr. Finlay to draw up a deed of gift, and when it's ready, this house and all that pertains to it will be yours.

JENNY. If my father had meant me to have it, he'd have left it to me.

ADAM. I don't know that he didn't mean you to have it, but whether he did or not, I do. You'll find the fortune almost as he left it. I haven't spent much of it . . . and perhaps you'll let me off that bit! . . .

JENNY (*impulsively seizing his hand*). Oh, Adam, don't talk like that! (*She begins to cry.*)

ADAM. You see, I'm not accustomed to large sums of money, and I don't want large sums of money. I don't know what to do with them, and wondering about them keeps me awake at night. I think to myself, almost maddeningly, oughtn't I to be doing something with all that fortune, but I can't think of anything. You see, I'm not really interested in the welfare of the world. I didn't make it, and I don't accept any responsibility for it. But there are plenty of people who are perfectly willing to act as God's deputy, and I don't mind them doing so, if they're fit for the job. All I know is that I'm not. What troubles me most is that the things I can do and like doing, aren't done because of the continual worry of my mind about this unused income. You're the only person, Jenny, who can,

I think, use this fortune as it ought to be used, as your father probably wanted it used, and so I give it to you, and I beg you, as an act of kindness to me, to take it. You will take it, won't you.

JENNY. Yes, Adam, I'll take it.

MRS. CORKEN. Is the world mad?

EDWARD. I begin to think it is. Ireland's been a lunatic asylum for the last twenty-five years. It's drivelling mad! . . .

MRS. CORKEN. Corner boys in the place of gentlemen. What kind of a country can you expect with the like of that going on? And you (*she turns to* JENNY), now you've got our money, what are you going to do for us?

JENNY. Oh, I'll see to you. My father had the burden of you, and I suppose I'll have to bear it, too.

EDWARD. Do you mean you'll give us enough to live on?

MRS. CORKEN. All I want is enough to die on.

JENNY. You shall have it.

FANNY (*rising*). I congratulate you, Miss Conn. Do you wish us to leave at once, or will it be convenient if we stay over the week-end?

JENNY. Can't we be friends, Fanny?

FANNY. I find it hard to adjust myself to so drastic a change in my life. You see, this was, I thought, my house.

JENNY. I know. But can't we be friends?

FANNY (*after a pause*). You must give me a little time!

JENNY. As long as you like . . . if you'll only be friends.

[FANNY *goes out, brisk as ever, proud as ever, gazing at no one, keeping her eyes steadily on the door through which she is to pass. She's a game woman,* FANNY!]

JENNY. Doreen, tell your mother not to hurry herself!

DOREEN. You mean we needn't go this minute?

JENNY. Uh-huh!

DOREEN. Oh, Jenny, darling. (*Hugging her.*) I wish you'd let me work for you.

JENNY. I will. As soon as I find out what you can do, I'll work you to death! (*She kisses the girl.*) Go 'long, now, and tell your mother.

[*Exit* DOREEN.

ARTHUR. I've drawn up a scheme for using a fortune!

JENNY. I know you have. But I have a scheme of my own. The sooner you start looking for a job, Arthur, the better.

ARTHUR. Jobs for people of my ability aren't easy to find. Besides, I'm going into politics! . . .

JENNY. Well, why don't you go?

MRS. CORKEN. Do you imagine any constituency will elect you to run the country when you haven't learnt how to run yourself? A nice thing, indeed, if a fellow that has never earned a penny-piece in his life was allowed to conduct a nation's affairs. But, sure, (*she gets up from her seat*) things are in such a state that it wouldn't surprise me if some place *did* elect you. Well, listen to me, boy, if you do go into parliament, get yourself elected in Eire, and not up here. You get more money in Eire.

ARTHUR. I'm not thinking of money! . . .

MRS. CORKEN (*who has been making her way to the door*). Och, away and divert yourself! What else does anybody think of? (*At the door, to* EDWARD.) Here you, come on! I want you to help me with that big suit-case of mine.

EDWARD (*getting up as he was bid*). Och, I'm no hand at packing things. I'm like yourself, I've never had to do things for myself.

MRS. CORKEN. Well, you can start learning. (*She goes out.*)

EDWARD (*to* JENNY). You meant that, didn't you, about giving us enough to live on?

JENNY. Yes.

EDWARD. Mind, just living isn't everything. It's the extras that matter. You'd hardly believe what a bottle of John Jameson costs these days.

JENNY. I might rise to one or two extras! . . .

EDWARD. Och, you've a heart of corn, you've a heart of corn!

[*He goes out, extremely pleased with himself.*

ARTHUR. I take it that no one wishes to consult me about anything? I'm the future, you know.

JENNY. I don't think so, Arthur. You see, we're the future, too. The very young aren't the whole of it.

ARTHUR. But we'll last longer.

JENNY. Will you? The past has lasted much longer than the future. The future hasn't lasted at all. It's only threatening to exist.

ADAM. And before it knows it's alive, it'll be the past. You're beginning to age yourself, Arthur. There's another generation on your heels.

ARTHUR. I have ideas, and ideas aren't too plentiful these days. You shouldn't disregard any suggestions even if you don't like the people who make them. I'll be in the garden if I'm wanted.

JENNY. Thank you for telling us.

[*He goes out of the French window.*

ADAM. I feel sorry for the young. Their ambition is so much greater than their ability. Would you like to be young again, Jenny.

JENNY. No.

ADAM. Nor would I. Youth's the unhappiest time of life . . . the age of impotent desire. I'm sorry, my dear, to have put this burden on you.

JENNY. I can bear it. I shall be able to do the things I've dreamt of doing. I've always had a longing to build a town.

ADAM. You haven't enough money for that.

JENNY. No. But if you can't build a town, you can build a village. And if you can't build a village, you can build a street. And if you can't build a street, you can build a house. I want to rebuild this one.

ADAM. Well, thank God I'm out of it all.

JENNY (*with a light laugh*). Are you? I wonder if you are.

ADAM. But of course I am. Clean out of it.

JENNY. What shall I allow you?

ADAM. Oh, please, Jenny, don't allow me anything. I'm not taking your money and leaving you to do the work.

JENNY. I can do the work all right. You see, I like it. And you have your own work to do.

ADAM. That's the work I want to do. I'm not fit to be rich.

JENNY. Are you fit to be poor?

ADAM. Nobody's fit to be poor.

JENNY. Except the saints.

ADAM. They aren't poor. They're the richest of us all. They don't need anything.

JENNY. You're a daft fellow, Adam.

ADAM. I suppose so. But I know what I want. The majority of people don't.

JENNY. Are you sure you know what you want?

ADAM. Absolutely. To be let alone to do my work.

JENNY. Do you know what I want?

ADAM. No. I sometimes wonder. What do you want?

JENNY. I want you.

ADAM. Do you know, there must be something very attractive about me. You're the second woman who has offered me her hand.

JENNY. The second?

ADAM. Yes, but I oughtn' to have told you that. Jenny, dear, I'm too old. Let me be a brother to you.

JENNY. Listen, you big stiff, I want you, *you!* (*She puts her arms round him.*) I wanted you the minute I saw you, that day the letter was read, and I've wanted you every minute since. I love you, you great big gumph, you!

ADAM. But I'm a perfectly useless person.

JENNY. I'll make use of you.

ADAM. That's just what I'm afraid of.

JENNY. I love you, Adam. Don't turn me down.

ADAM. I wouldn't dream of doing that, Jenny. You see, I'm very fond of you. But I've just got rid of the fortune, and if I marry you, I'll have it back again.

JENNY. Oh, no, you won't. I'll look after it. You see, I want to look after it, and nobody can look after anything properly unless he wants to. Just you go on writing your books, my dear. I'll attend to the fortune.

ADAM. Well, of course, as I said, I'm very fond of you.

JENNY. When you're fond of a woman, Adam, you kiss her.

ADAM. So you do. (*And he does.*) But all the same, I!...

JENNY. When a man's fond of a woman, he kisses her again.

ADAM. Yes, yes, he does.
        And he kisses her again.
        And that's the end of the play.